G. WILLARD COLLINS:
THE PEOPLE PERSON

G. WILLARD COLLINS: THE PEOPLE PERSON

Robert E. Hooper
and
Jim Turner

20TH CENTURY CHRISTIAN
2809 Granny White Pike • Nashville, TN 37204

20th Century Christian
2809 Granny White Pike
Nashville, TN 37204

Printed in the United States of America.
ISBN 0-89098-079-9

Dedication

To our Christian parents, Buford and Lorene Hooper and James and Marie Turner, who—like Walter and Maxie Collins—somehow found a way for their sons to learn and grow at David Lipscomb College. And to our Christian wives, Virginia Hooper and Elaine Hooper Turner, who—like Ruth Collins—have encouraged us to build on the Lipscomb Foundation.

Contents

Preface

Diogenes, the best-known representative of the Hellenistic Cynics, supposedly lived in a tub and carried a lantern wherever he went in order to search for an honest man. Evidently he was unsuccessful in his quest.

If Diogenes could have lived during the last years of the twentieth century, also an age of cynicism, he could have found an honest man in the person of Willard Collins. So honest, in fact, that he often has found it impossible not to tell everything he knows about any topic.

But Willard Collins is more than an honest man. He is a person who is universally liked, and by his closest associates, loved. Furthermore, he is bothered deeply when it seems that someone might not like him.

This loving character permeates everything Collins does. As vice president and president of Lipscomb, his greatest desire for the students has been to find their husbands or wives while in school. His preaching has always contained a sincere concern for his auditors. He loved them so much that it hurt him to think about some being lost eternally.

Closely akin to his radiating love has been Willard Collins' involvement with people. Everyone who has commented on Collins mentioned his interest in people—his ability to remember names and something about the person. His knowledge oftentimes did not stop with the person under discussion; many times he could relate family history at least back to grandparents. This knowledge of people extends throughout the friends of David Lipscomb College and the hundreds of churches where he has preached since 1934. The authors, therefore, have chosen to call this book *G. Willard Collins:*

The People Person. His success as a preacher and college administrator can be traced to this God-given talent. He is a friend to literally thousands of people because he is a caring person.

* * *

This book began as an idea in 1981. It was presented to the Faculty Summer Fellowship Grant Committee in 1982. They graciously accepted the proposal. I then asked my son-in-law, Jim Turner, to share with me the experience of research and writing. He readily accepted. It has been a cordial relationship throughout the production of the book.

Our approaches to writing are somewhat different. Jim is a feature writer, having spent many years as a writer and managing editor of two newspapers—the Russellville (Kentucky) *News-Democrat* and the Logan *Leader*. His experience as an English teacher at Russellville High School and presently at Logan County High School has added a needed dimension to the finished product. He was given the responsibility of reading the final draft.

I am more analytical in my writing. This is a result of my approach to the study, teaching, and writing of history. Thus the chapters of this book are somewhat different. We divided the narrative chapters equally, with Jim emphasizing the periods of Collins' life, including the family chapter. My chapters include his preaching experiences, his friends, and the presidency.

Jim and I have spent hours interviewing numerous persons who have willingly given of their time to make this book possible. Therefore, the end result has been an interesting experience for both of us. The book is basically oral history, although many documents were explored. The persons we interviewed are identified in the narrative. This book could not have been produced without their help.

President Collins gave us several hours of interviews, tapes that will be invaluable for future generations. In order to understand the family, we turned to Ruth Collins and the Collinses' two daughters, Carole and Corinne, and their families. All were quite open in sharing their perceptions of the family. Again, the book could not have been produced without their cooperation.

On campus, we have received help from administrators, faculty, and staff beyond what might be expected. When some factual information was needed, a call to the appropriate office produced the information within the hour. The staff of Crisman Memorial

Library has been very cooperative, allowing the use of sources outside the confines of the library. David England, director of the Lipscomb News Bureau, permitted us access to his files of newspaper articles, *The Lipscomb News*, and his library of photographs. We wish to publicly thank all who have been of such great help.

The oftentimes thankless task of typing and retyping of the manuscript was completed by Mrs. Jo Ann Harwell, secretary of the Department of History and Political Science, and Kimberly Redmon, an invaluable student secretary. We are certain that we have not stopped often enough to say "thank you" to both of them.

Both of us wish to thank our families for the support we received throughout the production of the manuscript. Virginia, my wife, and Elaine, Jim's wife, provided without complaint the opportunities for us to pursue our research and writing. I must mention two welcome distractions that prolonged the conclusion of the book. During the period, Jim and Elaine presented to us our first grandchildren, Clay and Lindsay.

REH
January, 1986

Chapter One

The First Grade Dropout

Had the student body of Bluff Springs School held a "Most Likely to Succeed" election in 1922-23, little Willard Collins might have finished dead last. In fact, the other children saw Willard so seldom that they hardly knew this tearful first grader, even though Bluff Springs was a rural, one-room school.

George Willard Collins gave little indication at Bluff Springs that he would so much as get past the first grade; in truth, he never completed grade one on a formal basis. A soothsayer bold enough to predict a four-decade career in college administration for this reluctant scholar would likely have been laughed out of the prophecy profession.

Yet this same primary dropout was destined to be one of the most outstanding alumni in the history of Marshall County High School in Lewisburg, Tennessee. He became one of the best all-around students ever at David Lipscomb College, earned advanced degrees at prestigious Vanderbilt University, and joined the ranks of nationally known college administrators, culminating his career in his service as Lipscomb's president.

"His mother would take him over to Bluff Springs School and leave him crying. Then she'd go home and cry for a while herself before going back after him. Finally she gave up on that and taught him at home that year. We didn't know whether Willard would ever go to school or not," confides his aunt, Mrs. Macel Collins of Lewisburg.

Over sixty years later, Willard Collins still turns up his nose when reminded of his Bluff Springs experiences. He says the school was too little and too far over the hill. "They took me there because that's where my mother and daddy had gone to school. I didn't like it," the college president explains without apology.

Trying another tactic to educate their only child, Walter and Maxie Collins bundled him into a buggy with his older cousin, Selene Collins, and sent him to the city school in Lewisburg. The first few days Mrs. Collins sat alone in the buggy during school hours, waiting to see if her little boy would need her. Soon he didn't.

"At first they'd drag him to school in that buggy. But when he got started to school, there was no stopping him," remembers Aunt Macel of her nephew, who has been in school most of the six decades-plus since.

There came a time a few years later when Willard still considered dropping out of school. As a sixth grader, he told his mother he planned to quit school after the eighth grade. She would hear none of that.

Maxie Duncan Collins had no intention of letting her boy, Willard, avoid an education. A traditional country woman who held a firm grip on the family's short purse strings, she always found the resources to provide her son the training usually reserved for children of wealthier, more cultured families.

"Mother always wanted me to have the best of everything," her loving son remembers. "She was trying to find my talents, I'm sure."

The thousands who have heard Willard Collins sing at church services or in Lipscomb's chapel might question if music is one of those "talents." Yet little Willard took piano lessons for seven years, beginning at the home of the woman who was to be his aunt, Macel Richardson. Then Maxie found funding for him to move on to twice-weekly training from townswoman Helen Bradley.

Probably the Collins' cultural-advancement funds were more properly spent on private drama and "expression" lessons from Bernice Cantrell, who was to be Willard's drama director and speech coach at Marshall County.

Frank Medearis suspects he even took a lesson in horseback riding on the sly. "I never had heard of 'posting' on a horse then. When Willard and I rode our ponies to school, I thought it was pretty funny how he was bouncing up and down on the saddle while I was just sitting there. Now I know he was posting to the rhythm of the horse and my pony was beating me to death," says Medearis, one of Willard Collins' closest childhood chums. Collins simply says,

"My daddy taught me how to ride."

Frank had ample opportunity to witness Willard's equestrian technique. Every day for years, the bib overall-clad boys rode their ponies almost three miles one way from Collins Hollow to Lewisburg to school. They survived the boredom of occasional dull classes by looking longingly out the window at their hitched horses, which were waiting to return them to the joys of their neighboring farms. At times Willard's parents paid for livery stable space for one of the three ponies which they entrusted to bear their pride and joy to school over the years.

The Willard Collins of sixty years ago that Frank Medearis remembers is much like the man college students and church congregations have grown to love and respect—the outgoing Christian with a booming voice and a zest for life. Yet in many ways the boy who so loved the great outdoors and its accompanying freedom had to be left behind on the doorstep of the college administration building.

In their seventieth years, both Willard Collins and Frank Medearis recalled vividly their boyhoods at Collins Hollow—days of farm work, baseball and football in the pastures, unrestricted small game hunting, and great adventures in the swimming hole.

Joining them were Frank's older brother, William Medearis, Jr., "a reader of books," and the Medearis' younger cousin, Harold Hayes, who was to die young as a military pilot. A four-year span separated William and Harold. In between were the leaders, Frank and Willard.

Those two still allow their eyes to dance as they recall diving into the pond for the sport of "fish grabbing." An unsuspecting fish would swim beneath a rock where three or four of the submerged boys would block the exits. Then someone would reach underneath the rock and pull out the surprised catch.

"We couldn't see what we had. Sometimes it would be a turtle or a snake. You'd learn to tell the difference by touch pretty quick," laughs Frank, his eyes still darting with childlike mischief.

In those days leading up to the Depression, the Medearis family treasury was a little more substantial than that of the Collinses, but that made no difference. The boys did little that cost money anyway.

"We'd play football or baseball just about every Sunday afternoon. We had mowed areas on either side of our house where we played. At Willard's, we'd have to go up on a hill to find a flat area,"

3

Frank remembers. "He and I were the catchers in baseball. Neither one of us ever wore a mask, but we never got hit in the face. He was a good athlete. We could—in fact, we did—run all the way to Lewisburg several times. We could have played sports at the school, but farm boys just didn't have the time."

Hunting ranked high on the list of favorite pastimes for the boys. Willard used a long-barreled 12-gauge shotgun his dad had passed down to him, and the boys were killing doves by the time they were 10. Squirrels didn't stand a chance with these guys. If the animals were playing hard to get, the young hunters would build a small fire in a hole under the tree and "smoke them out."

That love of hunting stayed with Willard Collins long after he had stopped running and catching. He took friends from Nashville, including Clay Pullias, on Marshall County hunting expeditions. He continued this for decades, until his eyesight prevented it about 1970. "He would take some of us from Old Hickory hunting at his parents' place after he began preaching," Paul Morrison recalls. "He called it 'squirrel hunting,' but he was so glad to be outside he'd shoot at the first thing he saw."

The boys played a few pranks, now mostly forgotten, Frank says. During their junior high days, a cow mysteriously appeared on the second floor of the Lewisburg School building on a Halloween evening. In fact, she made herself at home there until morning. Frank says he was the one punished for the escapade, explaining tongue-in-cheek, "Everybody knew Willard and my brother could do no wrong." "I have no recollection of that—no recollection," President Collins says.

Walter and Maxie Collins did everything they could to see that their child at least knew right from wrong. Maxie was a strong Christian woman. Although Walter did not always walk the straight and narrow as a young man and did not become a Christian until his son baptized him in 1935, he was a strict disciplinarian.

"In all the years I've known Willard and been so close to him, I never heard him say but one bad word," Frank says. "His daddy heard him, too. Mr. Dump slapped him down on the road right then."

"Mr. Dump" was the name Frank and the other boys used with respect for the man Willard called "Poppa." To most Marshall Countians, however, he was just plain "Dump Collins." The nickname came from his childhood when he was short and chubby. He outgrew the physical part of it, but the nickname stuck until his death in 1959 at age 74.

Walter "Dump" Collins came from a family of farmers who had lived for generations in the area still known as Collins Hollow (and pronounced "holler"). About 1850, Elisha Collins, Willard's great-grandfather, divided among his heirs some 840 acres of land in the area. One of his sons, Rufe, inherited a portion of it, which was again divided among his heirs, including sons Elisha ("Bud"), Walter ("Dump"), and Ed.

Had tradition continued, Willard, who would be the last of the male descendants bearing the Collins name, would have been called Elisha or Rufe, names which had adorned the family tree for generations. Instead he was named for another great-uncle, George. Where the Willard originated is not clear, although childhood friend Cobia Barron of Lewisburg believes heavyweight champion Jess Willard, who had won a 26-round thriller seven months before Willard's birth, had drawn Dump's fancy and gained a namesake, probably without ever being aware of the honor.

Dump Collins came from tough, frontier stock. Willard remembers an aunt picking up a snake in her bare hand and snapping its head off without blinking. Sometimes, Dump reverted to his rougher tendencies; at other times he was the model of decorum.

"He was a mess; that's what he was," lovingly laughs one of Willard's cousins, Ralph Nichols. "He had a way nobody else had." "He was just Uncle Dump, and that's all you could make out of him. He was a lot of fun," agrees Nichols' sister, Betty Garrett.

"My father-in-law was a delightful man to know. Willard's disposition and his ways came from his father," says Ruth Morris Collins, who married the Collinses' son in 1939. "When we'd go downtown in Nashville, he'd soon find someone on the street and strike up a conversation."

Mrs. Margaret Leonard Hopper, who served 35 years on the Executive Council at Lipscomb, is a native Marshall Countian. She knew the Collins family well and agrees with Ruth's assessment of Walter Collins.

"Willard has a lot of his father's traits. The first words his dad would say when he saw someone were: 'How are you? Come go home with me.' My father, William W. Leonard, was from an educated family, but he and Mr. Collins could talk with each other well," Mrs. Hopper remembers.

Walter Marion Collins used his small bit of land to the fullest, trying earnestly to make a living for his family. During the summer months, the Collins men "swapped work," helping each other plant and harvest the crops. During the winter, Dump cleared land, grubbing bushes and chopping down trees, digging them up by the roots to make "new ground." He kept his fence rows clear, always the sign of a respect for the land and for oneself.

Over the years, Dump and Maxie Collins were able to rent a few acres to add to their farming enterprises. While Willard was still young, his parents used their savings to buy more land, increasing their farm to some 80 acres.

Walter and Maxie started as poor folks when they married March 7, 1909. The home where their son was born November 12, 1915, was a raised three-room, unpainted house that has been called a "shack." In the winter, the bath water in the galvanized tub sometimes froze, and Maxie kept her family warm in the uninsulated house with piles of blankets. Like their neighbors in pre-TVA days, they had no electricity and went many years without running water or indoor plumbing.

By the summer of 1929, by adding borrowed money to their funds, the Collinses built a new house where Willard's birthplace had stood. The family lived in the garage during the construction period. "The Great Crash and Depression came only a few months later. We couldn't have afforded the house if we had waited until then," Willard Collins recalls.

The Collins family could withstand the Depression better than many Americans. They had no investments except for the land. They raised their own food and were self-sufficient in many ways. They even found money to pay for Willard's private lessons in music and the communication arts.

* * *

Joe Tom Duncan, Maxie's younger brother, recalls that Dump was a one-day-at-a-time man. Given a home by his sister after their mother died young of pneumonia, Joe Tom often wanted to get the work done ahead of time so that he could pay his respects to the young ladies of the area. If Walter saw they were getting too far ahead with the wood cutting, though, he would tell Joe Tom, "Let's take a blow," signifying that a rest period was in order. Then Dump Collins would savor his favorite chewing tobacco.

Willard recalls that his dad engaged in very few laborsaving practices. "Poppa could always find the hardest way to do anything; he didn't believe in short cuts. I remember Poppa never took time to move a wagon load of corn from the barn by our house to the other farm. Instead, he'd pack corn on his back between farms one sack at a time daily. When we'd bale hay, we'd throw it in the loft loose and then throw it out later for the baler. It never occurred to him to do both jobs at once," fondly remembers the son, who sees all of this as part of his beloved dad's rural American work ethic.

Dump Collins had little formal schooling. Only because of his wife's influence was he interested in his son's education. In fact, he was in favor of Willard working fulltime at the H. G. Hill's grocery in Lewisburg after graduation rather than his going on to college. Yet Dump taught his son lessons he hasn't forgotten.

"He instilled in me the importance of hard work and honesty," Collins said half a century later in his DLC office. "I know where I plowed my first furrow after he had showed me how. I still remember his turning the mule over to me that first time. And I remember his holding up one of our neighbors as an example of a person who wasn't honest. 'You'll live to see him go broke,' he predicted, and the man did. He believed a man would pay for his dishonesty."

"A man of his word," was the way Athens Clay Pullias described Walter Collins in a *Gospel Advocate* tribute at the time of his death. "Honor and integrity were the very cornerstones of his personal life. His word was literally his bond. In an age of smooth duplicity and double talk, his straightforward honesty in speech and action stood out like the peak of a mountain."

Walter Collins did his share of disciplining his son. Little Willard often felt the brunt of a peach tree switch, especially if he gave in to the only-child tendency of throwing temper tantrums. "I must have done a lot of whining. My mother used to make marks on the smoke house wall every time I cried, and I remember a lot of marks. Poppa didn't let me do much of that around him."

Dump enjoyed a good time, though. Everyone liked him. He had a jolly nature that remains alive in his son. The first time Willard ever saw Nashville, the city that would become his home, came when his father hired cabby Steve Talley of Lewisburg and his taxi for a day. Talley drove Dump, Willard, and Ed Collins to the state fair in Nashville where a roller coaster ride made a lasting impression on the boy. "It scared me to death; I haven't been on one since," Collins laughs. Ed, who shared his nephew's opinion of the roller coaster, was like another father to Willard, especially since Ed and

Macel had no children of their own. Willard spent many hours at their home only two doors down the Collins Hollow Road, but when night came, Willard was expected at home.

"He'd hear his parents coming and start stomping around, claiming that he wasn't leaving, but Dump and Maxie saw to it that he was at home for the night," Macel Collins recalls.

Both Macel and her nephew remember Ed occasionally trying to tell his older brother how to rear the child. One day after Dump had disciplined his son, Ed followed his older brother to the barn and was heard to say, "You ain't got sense enough to raise that boy," but Dump took it all in stride. And he helped Maxie rear a special son.

Walter Collins faithfully attended worship services with his family, although he was not a member. He would stay outside during Sunday school and then sit on the back row with Ezra Barron. Willard, Harold, and the Medearis brothers most often sat on the front row, and Maxie had her place in the Church Street "A-woman Corner."

"Poppa listened to sermons on the radio at home, but he'd turn the volume down when he got sleepy," Collins remembers. "One morning he almost went to sleep at church when C. M. Pullias, Clay's uncle, was doing the preaching. He was sitting back there with his eyes closed, his hand winding the song book rack like a radio knob, trying to cut Brother Pullias' voice down. He always joked with C. M., 'I can't turn your volume off.'"

Maxie Collins, however, never slept in church. Described by all who remember her as a "fine Christian woman," she had few significant faults. Her brother, Joe Tom, says simply, "She was a good, strong Christian all the time. She never did anything wrong all her life." George Warren "Bud" Morris, Willard's brother-in-law, says if Mrs. Collins had a fault, it was that she "doted" on Willard too much. He was the light of her life.

"Willard was her life. She gave him every advantage she could. She waited on him hand and foot, drawing his bath water and putting out his clothes for him until he was grown," Ruth Collins says of her mother-in-law, adding that Maxie's act was a hard one to follow for a young bride.

Margaret Hopper remembers Maxie Collins well: "She was a quiet, demure, fastidious, neat, organized woman who was thoughtful and thorough. She dressed well, using her money wisely for quality clothes at the best store in Lewisburg. She always saw that Willard had the best, too. And she was a wonderful cook. She always had excellent meals, tastily prepared."

In addition to being the family's budget director, Maxie worked hard. She raised chickens and paid the grocery bill with proceeds from her sales of eggs and garden produce. Her son and other members of the Lipscomb faculty, particularly Dean J. P. Sanders, got their "nice white" eggs weekly from Collins Hollow many years after Willard had moved to Nashville.

With his mother and father setting the example, young Willard Collins learned to join them in farm work. "Willard was a worker. He worked hard on the farm—cut wheat, plowed corn, and took up hay," remembers cousin Ralph Nichols. He milked cows morning and night, even during the school year, and he spent a lot of time gathering eggs, including under the kitchen, where snakes often dwelled.

Willard presented quite a sight as a working child. Cobia Barron remembers the oversized gloves his friend wore. Willard recalls always wearing a big straw hat that was never secure on his head. "When I drove the team to thresh wheat, that hat would blow off and I'd take off running after it. I remember everybody laughing instead of being mad about work stopping," Collins recalls.

Most of the time, Willard and his dad worked alone. Sometimes when spring planting had to be done, Walter Collins would hire two men from Lewisburg, Rice Ewing and Grant McLean, to help. This provided a rare opportunity for young Willard to be around black people, as Collins Hollow was predominantly white. Since the schools were segregated, the only black child Willard was ever around was the son of a "washer woman" who helped his mother occasionally. He remembers dark threats his father made when the boy was bad about sending him up to the old slave quarters on a hill, which presented some type of mystical qualities to Willard. The threat was effective.

Threshing time in July was special. Even though the work was hot and hard, it was essentially a community social event, the type gathering Willard Collins still loves today. "We'd start at our house and everybody would help us. Then we'd move down the road to Charlie Bagby's, then to my uncle Bud's, to Ed's, and to Mr. Alf Richardson's, who was Macel's father," Collins remembers. "I'd get a dollar a day when we were at somebody else's farm, but what I remember best is the big noon meals. The women would have a lot of food fixed. We'd go in and eat a lot and drink glass after glass of iced tea. Then it was tough to go out into the July sun with that cold tea in you. I'd be the first to have to unload my wagon, but it was community work and I looked forward to it."

The last day Willard wcrked in the field was in 1933. His parents had put together enough money for him to take a dream trip in the summer before his senior year in high school. One of his teachers, W. J. Moore, and three other boys, Charles Miller and Oscar and Frank Boyd, trekked to the Chicago World's Fair and points far beyond.

After witnessing the "Century of Progress" theme at the fair, they headed east, visiting Boston, Plymouth Rock, Niagara Falls, New York's Coney Island, and Washington, D.C. returning to Marshall County three weeks later, a great deal more sophisticated and a little worn out from taking turns riding in Mr. Moore's rumble seat.

The farm boy had become "citified." He was never to put the harness back on the mule again. Nichols remembers his cousin coming home as a college student one time to help his dad. "His hands were so tender that a pitchfork made blisters on them. He almost got blood poisoning from it," Nichols says. "I might have been satisfied farming all my life, had I not known anything else," the college president reflects half a century later.

Walter Collins helped his son get a job working Saturdays at the H. G. Hill's store in Lewisburg for manager Wilson Beech. Willard worked there fulltime the summer after his graduation from high school before some Christian people influenced him to attend David Lipscomb College, much to Maxie's delight.

Work and family were far from the sum of Willard Collins' existence, and he was a success in virtually everything he tried. He recorded outstanding achievements in school and showed unlimited potential as a young member of the Church Street Church of Christ in Lewisburg.

As a youngster, Willard was respected by the adults of the congregation. He, along with the Medearis brothers and Harold Hayes, always sat at the front of the building during worship services without misbehaving. When people asked him what he wanted to be when he grew up, he quickly answered "a preacher."

All four of the boys were baptized in Church Street's indoor baptistry on the same night in 1927. Strangely enough, Willard's uncle, Ed Collins, and a cousin, Marcus Turner, responded to the invitation that same evening at the rural Bluff Springs congregation. Willard can't recall whether he had talked with Ed about his plans to be baptized that evening or not. The boy who was so close to his family, especially his uncle, might have played a role in their response.

Although he has a clear memory of so many other details of his youth and of his career as a minister, President Collins cannot recall the date of his own baptism. He says legendary evangelist Foy E. Wallace, Jr. was preaching that night in a gospel meeting at Church Street. Jack Batey, one of Willard's school teachers, and a member of the congregation, baptized young Collins. Batey's son, also called Jack, began teaching at Lipscomb while Collins was a student, and his daughter, Irma Lee Batey, was a long-time member of the Lipscomb music faculty while her fellow Marshall Countian was an administrator.

While details of his baptism are unclear, there is no question that Foy Wallace had a great impact on Willard Collins' desire to become a preacher. Both Wallace's delivery and the message he brought had impressed the boy. "I've always thought that Willard, who had a competitive and success-oriented nature, was impressed by the acclaim a gospel preacher could have when he saw Foy E. Wallace, Jr., in action," says Bud Morris.

Wallace was later to be a part of a confrontation at Church Street which made a vivid impression on Willard Collins as a youthful member of the church. Collins since has been a witness to and often a mediator in similar church-dividing struggles.

* * *

Collins' first experience with church division came not long after he had been baptized. A segment of the congregation rebelled against the eldership's reluctance to employ a fulltime preacher. Wallace, editor of the *Gospel Advocate*, and David Lipscomb College president H. Leo Boles came to Lewisburg to discuss the situation on a Sunday morning. Members of the congregation took a vote which led to the ouster of the existing eldership, and young Willard was one of those casting a vote to choose new elders. The scene wasn't a pleasant one. Church Street, Lewisburg's largest religious body, was divided with a second congregation being organized. "The hardest thing I've had to reconcile all my life is when an issue becomes so important that it is worth splitting the church over," the Lipscomb president says.

While Church Street was in a quandary about its overall direction, many members of the congregation recognized the leadership potential of young Willard Collins. A few of them were sitting around the stove in the basement of the church building one cold Wednesday evening when Willard spoke for the first time in a service. Banker R. L. McBride was there. He doesn't remember the subject and neither does Willard, but McBride recalls knowing then he was hearing a young man with great potential.

Lewisburg youngsters had excellent Bible teachers in Ben Derryberry and Mayfield Ledbetter. A 1932 picture of the class shows Frank Medearis on one side of their teacher with Willard on the other. Harold Hayes is beside Frank. Also shown were Thomas Barnett, Eddie Woods, John A. Wheatley, Paul Turner, Ed Rutledge, Robert Kincaid, J. W. Hooten, Fowler Gupton, B. D. Thrasher, Cobia Barron, Clyde Lowe, Tillman Woods, Thomas Shaddy, Leon Coffman, John Andrews, Jr., James Beckham, Bill Lowe Wheatley, Roy Derryberry, R. G. Collins, James Orr, Carl Talley, Bill Pigg, and Murrey Wilson.

By then William Medearis was already in college. In fact, two members of Ledbetter's class, in addition to Willard, became college educators. William became chairman of the Bible Department at Alabama Christian, and Murrey Wilson joined the Harding University faculty. Evert Alexander, who also studied with them at Church Street, became the fourth minister in the group.

Among his countless honors, one President Collins cherishes most is having served as Secretary of the Sunday school at Church Street Church of Christ. W. M. Carter, editor of one of Marshall County's newspapers, the Lewisburg *Tribune*, was Sunday school superintendent. Felix Hayes, Harold's father, chose the teenager with the booming voice to speak to the entire congregation at the end of each Sunday school session for a year, reporting statistics and giving other data about the classes. In addition to this being an honor, the role gave the future preacher experience in addressing a congregation.

Another newspaperman played a big part in Willard Collins' life, too. Jim McCord, publisher of Carter's rival, the Marshall *Gazette*, was an accomplished speaker with great stage presence. He was so good at moving audiences that he was later elected governor of Tennessee. "I modeled my speaking style after Jim McCord's. I heard him often; in fact, he spoke at my high school commencement. I guess if I hadn't gone to Lipscomb I might have become a lawyer, and Jim McCord would have gotten me involved in politics. He was pointing me that way," Collins reflects.

As a youth, Willard and his parents were on hand virtually every time the doors opened at Church Street, but that was contrary to the way things had been when he was a child. "When we went to Bluff Springs Church of Christ, we missed a lot of Sundays," he recalls. "There were no Sunday evening or Wednesday services, and we didn't think much about it if we didn't go every Sunday morning. Our family visited a lot. The aunts and uncles would come see us or we'd go see them on Sundays. If Kate and Charles came from Mooresville before church time, we'd stay there and cook, eat, and play. Those were horse and buggy days. I don't think missing services is right, but we were in a different culture then."

Both Walter Collins and his wife-to-be, Maxie Duncan, were reared in the church, or as Joe Tom Duncan puts it: "The Duncans and the Collinses were turned to the Church of Christ always." The Duncans were from Wilson Hill, where the Church of Christ had its Marshall County roots when the legendary Barton W. Stone did evangelistic work there. "I've often wondered what my life would have been like if Barton W. Stone had not come to Wilson Hill," says Collins, who developed an evangelistic style and effectiveness that would have made Stone take notice.

The Duncans were probably more diligent in church work than were the Collinses, although after becoming a Collins, Maxie set a better example for her father, Lum Duncan, than he did for her. Willard remembers going to Grandfather Duncan's funeral, but nothing about the man. He remembers his paternal grandmother, "Miss Sallie" Collins, as a strong country woman who worked hard in the fields in her long dresses and who shared the love of family, but he admits, "I never remember Grandma going to church."

Just as there was nothing in his early life to predict that Willard Collins would become a college administrator, there was little to suggest his family would produce a powerful preacher.

Collins now feels he was fortunate to have weathered what could have been an influence to leave the church or at least not preach. He remembers his teenage girlfriends were not members of the Church of Christ.

When I was a sophomore in high school I went with a girl, Mary Gillespie. She lived at Burlin and was a Methodist. I used to go to young people's meetings with her on Sunday nights. I don't think my mother and daddy minded that much, even though I had been baptized. I dated Doris Bryant, another Methodist, and Annie Ruth Gates. I don't believe I had ever gone with any girl who was a member of the church when I finished high school. I don't remember anybody talking to me about the need to date a girl who was a member of the church. Now I know that's how you get weaned away.

While he was maturing as a Christian, Willard Collins was also being recognized as a good student with unlimited leadership potential and skills in a wide variety of extracurricular activities. He was elected president of his freshman and senior classes at Marshall County High. As a sophomore, he was one of three class leaders selected to meet regularly with the Rotary Club. When he was a junior, he was the class journalist, reporting for the school newspaper, the Marshall *Mirror*, beginning a long association with the print medium.

In his senior year, honors poured in for the boy from Collins Hollow. He served as class president; Harry Allen, Martha Harris, and Frances George were his fellow officers. He was chosen as one of the three top seniors in the categories Best All-round Student, Most Versatile, Most Useful, and Most Popular Boy. His schoolmates named him as the school's most outstanding boy, the equivalent of Bachelor of Ugliness, an honor he later won at David Lipscomb College.

"We were very political then, and it was usually the city kids against country kids. All of our little communities would get together. We could win almost anything, and I was usually the country candidate. . . .The same thing happened at Lipscomb. It was boarding students versus day students, and there it was the boarding students who could get elected. I'd learned that at Lewisburg."

Willard was also president of the French Club and a member of the Glee Club. In fact, he was the bass for a quartet which included Carl Talley, Folk Lambert, and Shelton Henderson; Collins Hollow's star football player sang at the football banquet his senior year instead of being honored as a Marshall gridder. His singing, which can fill a room in much the same way as his speaking, remains a distinct memory of chapel for many alumni. He has not been asked to lead congregational singing often, he admits. Activities that involved speaking more than singing were the ones in which Willard Collins excelled. He became an excellent debater, teaming with John H. Gillespie as a powerful negative team that finished second in a tournament at Murfreesboro. He was an accomplished actor, and Miss Cantrell, who had taught him publicly and privately for years, cast him in productions whenever possible.

His greatest memory as a high school speaker came from his winning among seven competitors in the Marshall County Declamation Contest. He not only won the McCord Medal but earned the right to speak on the theme "Dreams of American Democracy" at the Little Tenn declamation contest in Springfield, far on the other side of Nashville. The regional contest was aired over powerful radio station WSIX, a major step for a youngster who wanted to make a career using his voice.

Willard was the student speaker at the opening of the new Marshall County High School auditorium May 25, 1935. Lewisburg newspapers said he "eloquently" expressed the students' appreciation for the beautiful new facility.

One honor that escaped Willard was academic leadership of his class. "Mother really wanted me to be valedictorian, but Charles Miller got it and Frances George was salutatorian. I finished third among the 33 seniors," he remembers, still shaking his head a little over disappointing Maxie Collins.

To take part in all of his activities, Willard had to stop riding his ponies to school and find better transportation. "I rode to school on the Borden's Milk truck when Dick Barnett came through to pick up the milk Poppa and I had gotten each morning. I'd ride with him in the mornings. In the afternoons Mother would be waiting for me in our 1928 Chevrolet after I'd practiced for a play or a debate. She was always there when I needed her," her son recalls over a half century later.

Mrs. Collins was the main driver in the family, although Willard often had the use of the car at night. Dump Collins never wanted to learn to drive. Cars and doctors were two of his least favorite things. The first night he ever spent in the hospital came the day before his death after he suffered a major stroke in January of 1959.

Ironically, it was in a Marshall County automobile accident on November 22, 1963, that Maxie Collins died, almost at the same moment that President John F. Kennedy met his death in Dallas, Texas.

Willard was always interested in transportation. Uncle Joe Tom remembers him as a toddler "driving around" the kitchen of his childhood home, using a plate as an imaginary car. One of Willard's earliest recollections is of a toy car he won, and of his having a little boy argument with his cousin, James Brown, over a wagon.

His Aunt Macel recalls Willard's leaving his team of mules standing in harness while he went running toward an adjacent field where an airplane, a rarity in Marshall County in the twenties, was making an unplanned landing. "I've got to see that airplane," he yelled back to his shocked father.

It was an automobile ride he took with R. L. McBride and Sam Crutcher in the summer of 1934 that changed his life.

* * *

McBride, an elder of the Church Street congregation, took Collins to the David Lipscomb College campus for the first time, obtained financial aide for him, and helped him enroll in the Nashville junior college. The long-time bank president and Church Street elder says introducing Collins to Lipscomb is one of his most cherished memories.

Strangely enough, Willard and his family had never talked about his attending David Lipscomb College, even though the boy was a strong student, a good church worker, and an aspiring preacher. The Collinses were familiar with Lipscomb because of the preachers who often came to Marshall County from the school, but had not seriously considered it for their son.

Credit for initiating the idea of Willard Collins becoming a Lipscomb student goes to a young woman who helped change the course of DLC history. "I was standing in line to graduate from high school when Sara Whitten came up to me and said I ought to go to David Lipscomb College. That's the first time I had thought about it," Collins remembers.

Actually the girl's name was Sara Woodward then. A native of Farmington in Marshall County, she had completed high school two years earlier and had just graduated from Lipscomb, then a junior college. She later was to teach at David Lipscomb while Collins was vice president and president. Mrs. Whitten became widely known as a regular panelist for 17 years on the Nashville television show *Know Your Bible,* a program which Willard Collins helped originate.

"I had heard him speak and realized that he had great talent," Mrs. Whitten says. "I made a point to find him in line, told him I had been to Lipscomb for two years, and said he should go there. I told him Lipscomb was 'heaven on earth.' If I never did anything else, that's my claim to fame, introducing Willard Collins to Lipscomb."

Willard had been wavering on his long-announced intentions of becoming a minister. He was thinking about studying to be a lawyer, and probably would have attended Middle Tennessee State College had not Mrs. Whitten approached him at graduation. The scarcity of money, though, made his immediate enrollment in any college seem virtually impossible.

"Times were hard in the summer of 1934. I had just about decided not to go to college, maybe to work a year at the H. G. Hill's store and then try to go to school. I knew about Lipscomb, but I don't guess I'd thought much about coming here," Collins reflected while sitting in the president's office 50 years later. "My daddy would have liked for me to have worked at the store. Mother wanted me to go to college, but we didn't have the money."

After Sara had given him the idea, Willard became keenly interested in attending Lipscomb when he was "recruited." Miss Ora Crabtree, the well-known director of speech and drama activities at Lipscomb, drove to Lewisburg to ask him to come to DLC and become involved in her program. Collins was thrilled with her interest in him as a speaker. He told his parents that Lipscomb was for him.

Dump Collins wanted the best for his son and he wanted to please his wife. He went to discuss the matter with McBride at First National Bank. Several leaders of that bank were members of the Church of Christ. In fact, President Will Fox had been present that winter Wednesday when Willard made his first talk at church. "Willard's dad wanted the boy to go to Lipscomb, but he wasn't financially able. He asked if I could help," says McBride.

Instead of arranging a loan, McBride drove Willard and Roy Derryberry, one of his classmates at Church Street and Marshall County High, to the Lipscomb campus on a day that McBride's father-in-law, Sam Crutcher, had a doctor's appointment in Nashville. McBride drove Mr. Crutcher's Buick up Highway 31-A with the two boys in the "mother-in-law" seat in the back.

When they arrived at Sara Whitten's "heaven on earth," McBride took the prospective students to the administrative offices. The banker recalls arranging Willard's enrollment with a bright young teacher on the DLC faculty, Athens Clay Pullias. Collins doesn't remember meeting his long-time associate that day. Instead it was a visit with the school's new president, E. H. Ijams, that made an impression. Ijams had just assumed the presidency after Batsell Baxter had returned to the Abilene faculty.

By the time they headed back to Marshall County, Willard Collins was enrolled at David Lipscomb College with the promise of enough work on campus to make his attendance financially feasible. Roy Derryberry was also enrolled.

"I was surprised to hear Roy was going to Lipscomb because he wasn't planning to be a preacher, and we thought of Lipscomb as a place preachers went to school. I sure wasn't surprised about Willard. He always wanted to be a preacher, and I knew he could do and be anything he wanted," Frank Medearis says.

Roy Derryberry left school early in his freshman year. Willard Collins cast his lot with David Lipscomb College for a lifetime.

Willard at a young age

Walter "Dump" Collins

Willard and Maxie Collins

Chapter Two

The Editor and Orator

"The Editor and the Orator look like a pretty good couple to me."—*The Babbler*, March 14, 1935.

The Willard Collins who appeared in Nashville in 1934 was a well-rounded college student, one of the best David Lipscomb has ever known. He was a success in the classroom, in extracurricular activities, at the ballot box, in social life, and as a proponent of the Christian life.

Yet half a century later, most of his peers from his college years recall Willard primarily for three things—his ability as a speaker, his association with teacher Athens Clay Pullias, and his constant companionship with a peach of a young woman from Georgia named Ruth Morris.

Instead of being a speaker, Ruth Morris became adept at using the written word. The woman who later became Mrs. Willard Collins had already been a Lipscomb student a year when the boy from Collins Hollow arrived. She became editor of the student newspaper, *The Babbler*, when Willard was a freshman at the two-year school.

"'Ah, *The Babbler*!'", Dr. Jim Thomas, currently the Assistant Vice President for Campus Affairs and Dean of Enrollment, remembers Collins saying with fervor and gusto in the late sixties. "I was a reporter for *The Babbler* and my editor, Kenny Barfield, asked me to take a story for Brother Collins to see. When I mentioned *The Babbler*, I was impressed with how excited a college vice president was about the student newspaper."

Anything that enhances the lives of students at DLC always excites Willard Collins. Yet he holds a special place in his heart for *The Babbler*, and not just because he served as its faculty advisor for a few years.

It was *The Babbler*, you see, which brought Ruth and Willard— the Editor and the Orator—together. Lipscomb, in the throes of the Great Depression, had been without the finances to publish a paper in 1933-34. Under the leadership of Dean Norman L. Parks, *The Babbler* received a trial run the following year, under the conditions that it must support itself through advertisements and subscriptions. Frank Pack was to be editor-in-chief with Ruth school editor. J. W. Stutts, Jr., accepted the position of business manager. By winter quarter, however, Ruth had become editor and Stutts had moved into the advertising manager slot. A farm boy from Marshall County named Willard Collins was the business manager.

"I didn't like that job because I had to spend too much time on the street car. The printing was done downtown, and if a late story or ad came in, it was the business manager's job to take it down there to get in the paper," Collins recalls. "My daddy didn't like it either. He'd say, 'Law me, I sent you up there to go to school and all you're doing is riding that street car.' I got out of the job as soon as I could."

The street car treks, though, earned Willard a bus ride to Cookeville for a three-day conference at Tennessee Polytechnic Institute. The Tennessee Collegiate Press Association was being formed; the editor and the business manager represented Lipscomb. Both deny they planned the trip to get better acquainted.

"I knew I wasn't going on that trip by myself with him. So I got Jewell Parsons, a girl who lived in nearby Celina, to ride with me," Mrs. Collins remembers. "I stayed in the home of Professor Thomas Passons, a teacher at Tech, the organizer of the press association. I do remember walking around town with Willard, though, and I guess you could say when we got back we were going together."

"On the way down, I rode on one side of the bus while Ruth and Jewell sat on the other side," Collins recalls. "But when we came back, it was Jewell who was on the other side. Ruth and I were together then, and I guess we have been ever since."

Ruth had been a popular date among Lipscomb's bachelors. As a freshman, her escorts had included students Melvin Carlton and

Eugene Boyce, the future "Fessor" of the Lipscomb athletic department. "The first time I ever heard of Willard Collins was in a letter Melvin got while we were roommates at Harding in the spring of 1935. It was from Ruth, telling about her new romance," Boyce remembers.

"Ruth had dated many people, but I never felt she would marry one of them. I never doubted that she would marry Willard, though," says Ruth's childhood friend and Lipscomb roommate Eugenia Hart Smith.

Wherever Lipscomb couples gathered in 1935 and 36, Willard and Ruth usually appeared. Coach Bob Neil and his bride Martha often served as chaperones on the Lipscomb social scene. They had one of the few cars on campus, and Neil recalls how "close" Willard and Ruth were.

Mildred Finley Edwards remembers that she and her late husband, Paul Edwards, often double-dated with the future Mr. and Mrs. Willard Collins. "We would walk to Radnor Lake and back, or over to Reservoir Park. The longer the walk, the more the fun," Mrs. Edwards recalled August 9, 1985, while being inducted into Lipscomb's Golden Circle with Ruth and other members of the class of 1935. "I lived in Sewell Hall our second year, but some weekends I would go home and Ruth would visit me. Paul and Willard would come see us. Those days were so much fun!"

Ruth Morris' arrival on the David Lipscomb College scene had been as unplanned as was her future husband's selection of colleges. She had earned academic and extracurricular honors at Girls' High in her native Atlanta after getting her first journalism experience on the *Joe Junior* staff of Joe Brown Junior High School. Four years of Latin aided her writing, and she was equally good at mathematics. She tried unsuccessfully to win a math scholarship to Vanderbilt University.

Her parents, Franklin Paul and Mae Bearden Morris, were not able to pay tuition for their daughter, since the Depression had wreaked havoc with Morris' construction business. "He was the most successful contractor in Atlanta; he had a Cadillac with a rumble seat," says Madison Church of Christ minister Jim Mankin, a native of Atlanta. "But the Depression destroyed his business. He was lovable, real good with children. We called him 'Uncle Paul.' I've always been told, though, that he never got over the Depression."

Mae Morris was born in Nashville where her father, O. D.

Bearden, was a leader of the church. He later helped establish the first noninstrumental church in Atlanta following "the split." Mrs. James A. Harding, the wife of the co-founder of the Nashville Bible School which became David Lipscomb College, was a teacher in the Sunday school at the Morris' home congregation. The preacher there was a close family friend, B. C. Goodpasture, who became the long-time editor of the *Gospel Advocate*.

"The only preacher I ever really knew before coming to Lipscomb was Brother Goodpasture. I adored his wife, Cliett's mother," Mrs. Collins says, referring to J. Cliett Goodpasture, who was to become a vice president under her husband at DLC.

B. C. Goodpasture had been the preacher at the West End congregation in Atlanta several years before taking a position in another state. Meanwhile the church in Atlanta was growing and the need for another congregation in the city arose. Ruth's father and her Uncle George constructed the building for what was then called the Seminole Church of Christ. Today it is the widely known Druid Hills congregation. Goodpasture returned to Atlanta to be the preacher and Paul Morris was one of the deacons.

Ruth's grandfather Bearden was doing mission work all over Georgia. "Poppa," as Ruth and the other Morris children knew him, started congregations throughout the state.

Grandfather Morris had died when Ruth's father was only nine years old, causing the boy to have to go to work as a child. His mother lived until 1933, Ruth's senior year in high school, and reared her sons in the church.

In the summer of 1933, famed evangelist and educator S. P. Pittman was conducting a gospel meeting at the East End congregation in Atlanta, and the Morrises attended. He knew the family well and was aghast when he learned of Ruth's considering Vanderbilt instead of Lipscomb. Before the revival had ended, Pittman had arranged a full work scholarship at DLC for the girl. Taking no chances, he bundled her in his car along with song leader Richard Maxwell and took her back to Nashville with him.

It was a year before Willard Collins found himself in the R. L. McBride vehicle headed for Nashville, but the die was cast for one of the great partnerships of all time.

"With the orator and the editor side by side, no obstacle shall be too big for them to surmount," aptly predicted *The Babbler* of May 2, 1935 while naming Ruth Morris to its Hall of Fame.

Orator was an appropriate designation for Willard Collins. His speaking quickly earned him fame at Lipscomb when he won the Founder's Day Oratorical Contest as a freshman. An annual event commemorating the birthday of David Lipscomb in 1831, the contest ranks among the most prestigious prizes on campus and has always drawn many of the school's outstanding male speakers.

Twenty-four entered the 1934-35 competition. The group was narrowed to six who gave their addresses before a large radio audience over WLAC radio. Those six finalists speaking at the Central Church of Christ in downtown Nashville were Willard Collins, J. C. Moore, Jr., Jack Ezell, Joe Keller, Silas Triplett, and Jim Cope.

"People were so certain that Willard would win that George Cooper had written the story and the headline for *The Babbler* before the contest was even held," recalls George Warren "Bud" Morris, a David Lipscomb High School senior at the time. His sister, Ruth, was editor of the paper, but she has no recollection of the early story, since this was in January, a month before Willard Collins' actions became of supreme interest to her.

Willard's topic was "The Modern Frankenstein," a warning against man's growing dependence on mechanization. Professor Charles R. Brewer warned him against his theme, Bud Morris remembers, but that did not faze the confident Collins.

"In the course of time, the plot of the book *Frankenstein* has become a proverb: Beware of that creation which hastens the destruction of the creator. Tonight, in the 20th century, I point America to that proverb and warn them of a mighty fulfillment of the same in our native land," Collins told judges Sam Davis Tatum, Aileen Bromley, and F. Douglas Srygley, along with a regional radio audience.

"We are in the shadow of a great monster—I speak of that great iron monster, the machine, and the speed which our society is traveling to answer its mighty controls."

Lipscomb's appearances on WLAC, a station owned by alumnus J. Truman Ward, were welcomed throughout a wide area. People relied on the radio for entertainment during a pre-television age in which the economy kept people at home. President Ijams presided over the contest and the quartet of Bowling Boyd, Brantley Boyd, John Carter, and Elmer Duke entertained during breaks in the speaking.

As expected, when all was said and done, Willard Collins was wearing the Founder's Day Oratorical Contest medal. Fifty years later, many who were listening still vividly remember his voice and the "Modern Frankenstein" message.

Soon Willard drew a number of speaking assignments at Lipscomb. He was a student speaker at services of the College church, the forerunner of the current Granny White Church of Christ, which then met at Harding Hall on the DLC campus. A month after winning the contest, he spoke at the Wednesday service along with W. G. Mulligan, Ralph Autry, Paul Tucker, Bob Marrett, and Frank Pack, using themes from the first chapter of James. Those lessons were mimeographed and distributed for further reference.

At the Junior-Senior Banquet in Sewell Hall, Willard gave the Welcome Address, to which Senior Class President Richard Maxwell responded. He began appearing on Lipscomb's weekly WLAC show at the invitation of host Charles R. Brewer. His first appearance was in a skit about Abraham Lincoln as part of a cast which included fellow orators Moore, Cope, and Ezell along with Louise Thompson, John Campbell, Sidney Astin, and teacher Clay Pullias.

The orators became debaters. Lipscomb had gone without a formal debate team the year before even though Pack had some experience, and Lipscomb alumni Barrett Batsell Baxter and Norvel Young had enough talent and training to make the debate squad at Abilene Christian College. A varsity debate team, however, was reinstituted under President Ijams, who had also encouraged the rebirth of *The Babbler.*

Miss Ora Crabtree, S. C. Boyce, and Pullias selected the debaters. Boyce was the faculty advisor and Pack was a student coach, although Miss Crabtree did much of the coaching.

Selected for the team were Paul Crowder, Paul Edwards, Eugene Holloway, Harry Lee Moran, and "starters" Pack, Mary Ellen Evans, Jim Cope, and Willard Collins.

Willard was paired with Cope on a team of future presidents of church-related colleges. Cope, the best man in the Collins-Morris wedding, served as president of Florida College from 1949 until his retirement in 1982.

* * *

The debaters made DLC history by becoming the first non-athletes to earn college letters. After a *Babbler* editorial noting "Lipscomb is represented by others than those who compose athletic teams," letters were awarded after chapel in oratory and debate. Two were double-letter winners, Collins and Cope. Other lettermen were J. C. Moore, Joe Keller, Silas Triplett, Frank Pack, and Mary Ellen Evans.

Willard began achieving in a variety of ways on campus. His first mention in *The Babbler* came in the December 10, 1934, issue when Paul Tucker wrote in his "Religious Notes" column that Willard Collins had preached at Mooresville the week before. By the February 21 issue, Collins showed up in six different areas: debate, drama, preaching, journalism, speaking at the junior-senior banquet, and in a society column with Ruth. A January issue had recorded the academic Honor Roll for the first quarter and he had made that, too.

He was elected vice president of the Press Club, serving under the capable leadership of President Ruth Morris. He was named to the first Student Council of Elam Hall; Carney Nicks was chairman and Clay Pullias advisor.

Huge crowds turned out to see the pageant *Columbia's Concern for Her Country,* presented on May Day in June. The cast of students, faculty, and alumni included Willard in a role which proved to be prophetic as "Christian Education."

Politics entered into the picture, too. When the frosh arrived on campus, a group of Nashville students became class officers, led by Frank Womack, who had been president of the 1,000 students at Central High. It did not take Willard and others long to realize that those boarding outnumbered day students 187 to 70. (Enrollment included 94 seniors/ sophomores, 163 freshmen, and 166 in the secondary and elementary schools.)

"Day students had little time or opportunity to be involved in campus activities," remembers Word Bennett, a classmate of Willard's who became vice chairman of the college's board during the Collins administration and chairman of the committee seeking a successor for the retiring president in 1985. "This was still during the Depression, and we didn't have cars. We'd ride street cars to school, go to classes, and then go home or to whatever jobs we could find. I know I left the extracurricular activities to those on campus."

Willard and others decided that was a good idea. Just as the country kids had ruled at Marshall County, the boarding students took over at DLC. Under pressure, the original freshman class officers resigned. Elected in their place were President Robert Porter, Vice

President Warren Stough, Secretary Erin Hanlin, Treasurer Pat Lynch and Critic Joe Keller.

"Jim Cope and I led that [ousting of the old officers]. It's something I'm not proud of, and I don't think Frank Womack has ever felt as close to Lipscomb since; I can't say that I blame him. If students pulled something like that today, I'd kick them out," President Collins says.

Willard did little to detract from his reputation as a college student, though. One of his roommates, Bob Marrett, was involved in a prank of bringing a cow into the girls' dormitory, Sewell Hall, but unlike the incident at Lewisburg, no one believes Willard took part.

"Willard did have a very keen sense of humor and could thoroughly enjoy a clean joke or mischievous trick," recalls Alonzo Welch, who was in the class behind Collins at DLC.

Franklin Camp can attest to that. He and Willard became roommates and the closest of friends, an attachment which they resumed by long distance a few decades later. Camp remembers their getting in trouble once with Miss Martha Middlebrooks, the strongwilled head matron of Sewell Hall.

"We were assigned seats in the dining room in the basement of Sewell, three boys and three girls to a table, usually. Miss Middlebrooks would move us around after a few weeks so that we didn't become clanish," Camp recalls. "Willard knew I was ticklish, and he had one of the girls punch me in the ribs just as I reached for a dish. Gravy went flying everywhere, and Miss Middlebrooks wouldn't let us sit together at meals anymore."

Most people knew Willard as a serious, achievement-oriented future preacher ("Willard impressed me as being a very sincere minded and nonassuming young man, whereas now he has developed a more outgoing personality and a great sense of humor," fellow debater Pat Lynch says), but Camp knew the lighter side of his roommate. He recalls their taking a street car downtown for a movie on a hot Saturday afternoon, buying chocolate candy, and rolling with laughter when the chocolate melted into the hair of an unknown girl sitting in front of them.

"He enjoyed laughing as much as anyone I've ever been around. Once we had to leave the auditorium at the College church because we got so tickled about a strong-voiced girl holding the notes so long during the singing," Camp says about Willard, who has been known to hold a note himself from time to time.

Collins and Camp parlayed that humor into a column in *The Babbler* in the fall of 1935. It was called "The Greenhorns" with characters Nit and Wit telling their experiences as country boys in the big city school. Camp says the column was Willard's idea and was to be patterned after country comedians Lum and Abner. "You know Willard had to be Wit," Camp laughs.

"The Greenhorns" dealt with subjects like these: cafeteria food ("We get fly-back steak—stretch it, and it will fly back in your face"); Professor Charles R. Brewer ("I hope his face doesn't congeal when he's doing his apish look; when he began scratching girls' heads while telling about Gawain chopping off the Green Knight's head and mounting the radiator pipe on all fours, I began to think he'd had a swig of the real stuff"); Dean Parks (after a street car had "gone wild" on Caldwell Lane, the Greenhorns considered telling Parks about it but declined, realizing "he'd have to give us the history of the whole freight train"); and the Greenhorns' trips downtown to buy perfume at Woolworth's or to a movie where some of their real-life antics came to life on the stage.

Wit even penned a marriage proposal in the column with these romantic words in a poem:

After much meditation
And long consideration,
I have an inclination,
To become your relation.
If this declaration
Suits with your approbation,
I'll change your situation,
To a much better station,
Away down on the plantation.

Apparently that's as close to a proposal as Ruth ever got. "I don't remember ever making a formal proposal. I'd say we knew by the end of that first year we would be married," Collins says; Ruth shares that assumption. Camp did perform a mock wedding ceremony for the couple on the steps of Elam Hall in 1936.

"Ruth was terribly smitten. She never had any intention of letting Willard get away," says Bud Morris about his sister. Camp puts it: "She sort of set her eye on him and he didn't have a chance." Willard gave no indication he wanted "a chance" to get away.

When Willard began his second and final year as a Lipscomb student, alumna Ruth Morris was still on campus. She had taken a position as the school's first alumni secretary in President Ijams' office. The job involved spending countless hours with former two-term president H. Leo Boles and with S. P. Pittman, who had been on campus under all ten presidents after being a member of the first class in 1891-92. Those two helped her compile names of alumni, with whom she paired addresses to form mailing lists. Ruth also remained as editor of *The Babbler*, a title which became managing editor when senior Mary Ellen Evans became editor.

Ruth also kept a close eye on Willard, and she saw her (unofficial) fiance continue his string of successes. He became president of the Press Club, president of Elam Hall Student Council, a senior class officer, exchange editor of *The Babbler*, associate editor of the *Backlog*, and secretary/assistant to sociology teacher Athens Clay Pullias.

Additionally he became the first president of two newly organized groups, the Forensic Forum and the All Students Association. He was to revive the ASA when he became president of the college 42 years later.

Cope was vice president of the Forensic Forum with Miss Evans secretary. Other members included Cecil Allmon, Russell Johnson, Albert Gonce, Harry Holt, Edwin Norton, Alonzo Welch, Sidney Hooper, James Warren, D. T. Stanton, Joe Dennis, and J. R. McCord. S. C. Boyce continued as debate coach and Pullias was Forum Advisor.

"Although plans for the organization of an All Students Association had been materializing for some time, it was not until January 15 of this year that they were perfected, and the first president of the student body was elected, Willard Collins," the 1936 *Backlog* said without knowing what a significantly appropriate and historic choice the students had made.

Joining Collins on the first ASA Board were class presidents Warren Stough and Warren "Bud" Morris, senior class secretary Frances Keats, publication editors Evans and Carl Spain, Girls' Council secretary Erin Hanlin, Day Students' Club officers Claude Harris and Alberta Mitchell, and Jimmy Roy, who succeeded Willard as Boys' Council president.

The first big project for ASA proved to be great preparation for Willard Collins' future work. A massive fundraising campaign began to raise $350,000 to repay debts and for the construction of a library and the administration building, the location of Collins' office for four decades. Street cars bore placards asking for donations to Lipscomb, the Nashville Chamber of Commerce kept a "scorecard" concerning amounts given, Mayor Hilary E. House and Governor Hill McAlister proclaimed the first week in February "D.L.C. Week" with each giving personal contributions, and—under the leadership of Alumni Secretary Ruth Morris—bands of supporters were organized to solicit funds.

Willard pledged the ASA's support, saying, "Each individual must consider himself a representative of the school in every way that can be expressed. Especially must this be true at the convention held here February 4. Chapel will be attended by the visitors; this should mean good singing. Visitors will appreciate every courtesy."

The successful fundraising project met great needs in the forty-fifth year of David Lipscomb College, which had begun as the Nashville Bible School. Building-destroying fires in November of 1929 and March of 1930 had come only weeks after the crash of Wall Street, and the college almost had to close shortly before Willard Collins arrived on the scene. Faithful alumni, faculty, and friends had kept it going, but an infusion of money was essential.

The physical facilities of the school, which had moved to the South Nashville farm of co-founder David Lipscomb in 1903, consisted primarily of four buildings—Harding Hall, Elam Hall, Sewell Hall, and Burton Gymnasium. The girls lived in Sewell with the dining room in its basement. Men students and the families of some faculty members lived in Elam which had classrooms in its basement. Harding Hall had administrative offices, the elementary and secondary schools, and an upstairs auditorium for daily chapel services.

Between Willard's two years as a student, some improvements were made to the campus. The auditorium was remodeled to increase seating capacity to 229. The stage was raised, widened, and extended. Seventy new electric lights were installed and curtains added, which had to be pleasing to a young drama enthusiast like Willard. Eight rooms on the first floor of Elam were fitted for sixteen faculty offices. And a one-story frame structure just west of the gym was built to house a book store, a post office, and a cafe.

* * *

President Ijams' administration marked renewed interest in student affairs, as did Willard Collins' tenure four decades later. Ijams encouraged such student-centered ideas as the All Students' Association, the Forensic Union, and a rebirth of a mostly uncensored *Babbler*. Dr. James Cope fifty years later said "that paper covered what was going on in that school as well as any I've ever seen" under Ruth Morris.

The fundraising drive did not pay all the debts, nor did it finance future expansion. The administration building and library did not become realities until Willard Collins joined the Lipscomb Expansion Program almost a decade later.

Yet E. H. Ijams led a program which kept the school alive. Part of his success can be attributed to his boosting the Alumni Association by selecting as its first paid secretary the able Ruth Morris. In organizing the All Students' Association, Ijams was fortunate to have the energetic Willard Collins as its first president. The Ijams-Collins-Morris trio gave David Lipscomb College the kind of leadership it so desperately needed during perilous times.

The college Ijams, Collins, and Morris so dearly loved was Bible-based. In the famous deed which gave the farm of David and Margaret Zellner Lipscomb to the school, the Lipscombs stipulated that every student of the school must take a course in Bible every day. Additionally every student attended daily chapel services.

"DLC, requiring 30 hours of Bible for graduation, has the distinction of requiring more Bible than any other college in the world—junior or senior," *The Babbler* proclaimed in 1935. Lipscomb offered fourteen courses in Bible, at least one every hour of the school day. A 1936 *Babbler* maintained "all but one (unnamed) student in the college" was taking at least two Bible courses.

Willard was taking every Bible course he could to help him reach his ambition of becoming a preacher. During the fall of his freshman year, Willard wrote his mother—appropriately—asking her to help him find an appointment to preach his first sermon. D. D. Woody, a minister at Church Street in Lewisburg who was often invited by Collins in later years to speak at the Lipscomb Lectures, secured an invitation for young Willard Collins to fill in at Farmington in Marshall County on a Sunday in November, 1934.

The Farmington Church of Christ building must have been full that day. Many people attending a fiftieth anniversary observance of that sermon March 24, 1985, at Farmington recalled having been present. In that 1934 assembly were Mr. and Mrs. Walter Collins, Mr. and Mrs. Ed Collins, and a flock of their relatives.

Particularly interested was Sara Woodward (Whitten), the Farmington native who had encouraged Willard to attend Lipscomb. She remembers Willard—immaculately dressed as always—standing on a raised platform booming out his message. "There was no microphone, but he didn't need it," she says. "Everybody listened. Oh, he got attention! The predictors were confident that he would be a great preacher."

Collins does not recall what he spoke about in that first sermon. In fact, no one else seems to remember the topic. In 1935, he returned to Farmington with his topic "After a Year in the Pulpit: Where are the Christians?" Although his findings in that second sermon weren't recorded, Mrs. Whitten does remember what one of the listeners had to say about the first sermon.

"You find the truth among the country people. One of the older brethren said, 'You know, he's got a wonderful voice; if he ever learns anything to go along with it, won't he be a great preacher?'" laughs Mrs. Whitten.

It was the energetic voice and the personal magnetism of Willard Collins that attracted attention to him and continued to get him preaching jobs. Very little is remembered about what he said in those days, but the way in which he delivered the sermons continues to evoke memories.

"Brother Bearden, who was his wife-to-be's grandfather, kept saying so that anyone could hear it, 'Willard preaches too loud, doesn't he?'" says Jim Mankin, who has used many a Willard Collins story in his own speaking. Ruth's brother Bud recalls, "He was undoubtedly the loudest preacher I'd ever heard. The Seminole building was small, about the size of a duplex. He literally shook the rafters and our eardrums as well."

Morris does remember one of Willard's topics. The church at Celina decided to have an all-DLC service March 24, 1935, when Jewell Parsons brought several students home for a party. Morris was the song leader while James Reneau and Cordell Parsons led prayers. Willard was asked to preach.

"He talked on war, which I thought was a strange subject. Later I learned that had been the subject of Brother Pullias' sociology lectures that week," Morris recalls.

"What I remember about that is that Willard got sick while we were there," Mrs. Collins says. "We soon discovered he had the mumps; his face was really swollen. We took him home to Lewisburg, and he had to miss almost two weeks of school."

The preaching jobs continued for the budding speaker. He filled the pulpits of Catalpa Grove, Chestnut Ridge, Cane Creek, Mooresville, and many more.

Meanwhile he was hearing outstanding preachers at work in Nashville. The major addresses at the first Lipscomb Lectures he ever attended were along lines which proved to be important in his life. Freed-Hardeman College president N. B. Hardeman spoke on "The Christian College—It's Growing Importance." W. L. Oliphant, minister of the Oakcliffe congregation in Dallas, Texas, used as his topic "Evangelistic Work in the Modern World." Also on the program was Abilene Christian College president James F. Cox.

Willard was an active member of the Preachers' Club. Other 1935 members included Earl Aldridge, Cecil Allmon, R. L. Andrews, Sidney Astin, Ralph Autry, James Benson, Ed Bills, Franklin Boshell, J. W. Duncan, Paul Edwards, Fondren Fulford, Adolphus Grider, William Gentry, Robert George Goodall, Harry Hackworth, Woodrow Hicks, Chester Hogan, Jack Hutton, Eugene Holloway, Joe Keller, Carmack Keller, Elam Kuykendall, Ray McCord, Bob Marrett, Ed Norton, Frank Pack, Carl Spain, George Thom, Guy Tosh, Silas Triplett, Paul Tucker, Farris Vaden, Robert Vann, and Slayden Leathers.

In his senior year, the Preachers' Club, which was sponsored by John T. Hinds and J. P. Sanders, had as members: Allmon, Astin, Autry, Allen David Behel, James Benson, Boshell, Camp, Cope, Duncan, Bennie Lee Fudge, Albert Gonce, Fred Horton, Howard Horton, Joe Frank Hobby, Mac Keller, Kuykendall, Marrett, Norton, Henry Pyrtle, Howard Sain, John T. Smithson, Spain, Jim Tolle, Triplett, Vann, Woodrow Wasson, and Alonzo Welch.

Instead of returning to Marshall County at the close of his freshman year, Willard wanted a regular preaching job. Clay Pullias, whom Collins had served as secretary since January, played a role in finding him work. Pullias received a letter from John Cox, of the Jefferson Street Church of Christ in Orlando, Florida, concerning the congregation's need for an interim minister that summer. Pullias recommended Collins, and the boy from Marshall County had his first fulltime job.

Few years have passed that Collins hasn't been back to Florida to preach, often for that same church. When the congregation held its first service in its new building on Concord Street in 1963, Collins was the speaker. "One of the blessings of my life has been that the people I started with have stuck with me," President Collins said as he neared retirement.

Willard wasn't paid much by the congregation of fewer than 100 members, recalls member Mrs. E. A. Howard, but he gained the approval of the church. "He was always serious minded, yet he liked to have fun and soon made friends with the young people of the congregation," she says.

Howard Horton, chairman of the Bible Department at Lipscomb during the final years of the Collins Administration, was a freshman during Willard's second year. "I remember realizing then that he was already an established gospel preacher," Horton says.

Willard was becoming interested in holding meetings and in the success of evangelistic meetings. He wrote a bylined column in *The Babbler* called "So Others Say," which related what he was reading in other student newspapers. His lead item in his first column was about a meeting that famed black evangelist Marshall Keeble was having in Abilene.

"As always in Nashville, he is gathering hundreds of people every evening," Collins wrote. "In his own words, his audience hears what he says, 'gets hot under the collar, goes home, cools off, and comes back the next night for more.'"

President Ijams recognized Willard's ability as a preacher. He selected Collins and Jim Cope to represent Lipscomb at the third Rush Springs Lectureship in Oklahoma. Two student preachers from each of the Christian colleges spoke at the lectureship. Willard's subject was "The Modern Cry for Freedom" while Cope chose "Living the Life."

The prepared sermons were not judged; the competition was in extemporaneous speaking, where contestants had ten minutes to prepare a talk on the subject they had drawn. George Stevenson of Paducah, Texas, was the winner with Willard second among the ten speakers. Trine Starnes of Abilene Christian finished third, with Cope fourth.

The Oklahomans apparently liked what they heard from Willard Collins, since they asked him to speak a second time. He then addressed the subject "Are We Realizing the Significance of Sin?"

By the time he and Cope climbed back on the train to Nashville, Willard had accepted an invitation to return that summer to preach his first gospel meeting for the nearby Prairie Hill Church of Christ. In fact, he held meetings for that congregation five of the next six summers.

Collins doesn't remember who the first person was he baptized, although he feels certain it was a young man in Orlando. A baptism in the fall of 1935 may have been Willard's most meaningful. The elders of his home Church Street congregation in Lewisburg invited him to preach in September one Sunday before his second year at Lipscomb began. He had the joyful experience of baptizing his loving father, Walter "Dump" Collins. A cousin, Rufe Nichols, also responded to the invitation.

Walter and Maxie Collins got to see their only child win many more honors during his final months at Lipscomb. He was voted Bachelor of Ugliness (the equivalent of Mr. Lipscomb) by his fellow students with Howard Edwards and Robert Porter the runners-up. Frances Keats was Miss Lipscomb.

Willard was elected Class Orator and spoke at his commencement along with Walter H. Adams, dean of students at Abilene Christian. Collins' topic was "Undeveloped Possibilities of Youth." Boone Douthitt was the baccalaureate speaker.

"Willard's booming voice literally 'brought down the house.' The bleachers fell and several people were sent to the hospital," remembers fellow student Leonard Bradley. Actually the grandstand fell before the class marched into the area near where the high school gymnasium is now located, but it's the kind of Willard Collins story people love to tell and Collins loves to hear.

* * *

Willard's final weeks at Lipscomb closed with a flurry of dramatic activity with Miss Ora Crabtree apparently trying to get the most she could from the young man she had "recruited" to David Lipscomb College.

On May 15, 1936, he co-starred with Gertrude McClanahan in W. S. Gilbert's *Pygmalion and Galatea. The Babbler* said Miss McClanahan was "superb as a Greek statue coming to life" while Willard Collins—playing the title character—'put over his part in his usual fine, forceful style. Especially impressive were his soliloquies." Billie Craig played Collins' wife while other key actors were Cecil Allmon, Edith Caudill, Martha Lumsden, and Robert Vann.

Two weeks later Willard was in *The Brink of Silence* with William Marlin, Drake Macon, and Vann. Then in another two days, he was the Biblical David in *The Pilgrim and the Book*, a pageant directed by Miss Crabtree. Frank Pack played Pilgrim, J. P. Sanders was Revelation. Charles R. Brewer portrayed Satan, L. O. Sanderson was Moses, S. P. Pittman "rolled his R's" as Isaiah, and A. C. Pullias was Paul. L. T. Holland, Phillip Speer, E. B. Woodruff, and Miss McClanahan were in the cast, while Richard Maxwell directed a 48-member chorus.

"Miss Crabtree kept having Willard come back to be in plays while he was at Vanderbilt. She would tell President Ijams that I was the one who wanted him back, and he lectured me about it one day. I told him that she was the one, that I had rather he was working on his studies," Ruth Morris Collins remembers.

Ruth saw to it that Willard did his assignments at Vanderbilt. She spent many an hour in the library and in Kirkland Hall on the West Nashville campus helping him with research. A goodly portion of the $12.50 per month she was making at Lipscomb (plus room and board) went for street car money to take her to Vanderbilt.

Just how much of the schoolwork Ruth did ("That girl's getting your education for you," roommate Jack Dugger remembers telling Willard) is not clear, but she did her part of putting hubby-to-be through school.

"His handwriting was terrible. If he turned in handwritten papers, I'd ask him how he expected the professor to give him an "A" for that. He said, 'I hope they'd rather give me an "A" than try to read it.' But I would type a lot of his papers," Mrs. Collins says.

Collins' masters thesis at Vanderbilt under Dr. Walter Reckless was a statistical study of the tendency of released prisoners to become repeat offenders. He did extensive research, even eating with inmates at the Brushy Mountain prison. Ruth used her mathematical ability, which she had once wanted to apply as a student at Vanderbilt, to come up with statistical data for Willard's thesis.

"I remember one of my professors at Vanderbilt saying, 'I hope this Collins fellow stays on the right track. If he becomes a rabblerouser, we're all in trouble.' He was complimenting me for sticking with something until I got it done," Collins remembers.

Collins had become interested in sociology through his close association with Lipscomb sociology professor Clay Pullias. Willard had become his secretary/assistant/errand boy in January 1935, the start of an association which lasted forty-two years. *The Babbler* noted in the fall of 1935 that Pullias had published his *Outline Studies in the Social Teachings of Jesus* for use in a Bible class.

"Mr. Pullias was aided in the preparation of his manuscript by his wife, Frances Pullias, and his secretary, Willard Collins," the paper said, a statement which would apply to situations for decades to come.

"When I was in school here [at Lipscomb], Brother Clay Pullias would talk with me, and he'd talk about the dreams of A. M. Burton to make Lipscomb a four-year college. I remember one night we sat on the steps of Elam Hall—the side steps—and envisioned where buildings could be in a senior college," President Collins remembered fifty years later.

At Vanderbilt, Willard relied on Ruth. If Willard was doing the school work, she would help with the sermons, Dugger says. He can remember helping the young preacher memorize the supplemental material Ruth had gathered for a sermon.

Corinne Collins Slayton has heard stories of her mother helping in other ways, especially when Collins was a Vanderbilt student living at Lipscomb. "Girls weren't allowed in Elam, but every so often they'd block off the first floor of the dorm where Daddy always had his room and let Mother go in to clean it up for him."

One year, five Lipscomb alumni attending Vanderbilt lived upstairs in the home of a Mr. and Mrs. Way on Grand Avenue near the VU campus. Joining Collins and Dugger were Woodrow Wasson, Charles Black, and James Alexander. They got food as well as lodging there. "Mrs. Way was a product of the Old South and knew how to entertain in a grand way, although her cooking was generally better than the food she had to work with," Dugger recalls.

The boys occasionally took time for fun. Dugger remembers going used car hunting with Collins around Nashville. "Willard would race the motor. My job was to stand behind the car to see if it smoked. I don't think we ever bought one," says Dugger.

Dugger recalls how much he enjoyed getting his buddy ready to speak in the Sam K. Houston Oratorical Contest, Vanderbilt's equivalent of the Founder's Day Oratorical Contest. "He rented a tuxedo for the evening, but didn't have shoes to wear with it. I loaned him mine and we spit-shined them up for him. His daddy and mother came to see it, and I remember how Mr. Collins laughed about us fixing Willard up."

Willard finished second in the university contest to Wayne Dehoney. "He was a polished, smooth character whose mother was an expression teacher," Dugger remembers. "I thought Willard was great, but the other guy was awfully smooth. My guess is that Willard didn't modulate his voice enough. He may have been too loud."

Willard Collins was using his voice for greater things. He had regular appointments every Sunday at some congregation in the area. In the summers he was going back to Orlando and preaching meetings in Oklahoma and elsewhere.

Then came his first Nashville meeting; it was at the Eleventh Street Church of Christ and came through an invitation from E. F. Bigger, a native of Chapel Hill near Lewisburg. Willard shocked Nashville by baptizing fifty-four and restoring thirteen in that spring of 1937.

Word of that work was announced daily over WLAC radio on the Central Church of Christ's radio program by minister E. W. McMillan, who had succeeded the legendary Hall L. Calhoun at the start of Collins' second year at Lipscomb. "Who is Willard Collins?" people wanted to know. They soon were to find out.

"Willard would come home from preaching at that meeting really whipped, he'd be so tired from school and preaching," Dugger remembers. "But even at that time he knew exactly what he was going to do with his life—he was going to be a great evangelist."

Ruth seldom went with her fiance to his preaching appointments. "Willard didn't feel that it looked right," she says. Collins explains, "One of the brethren had called me off early in my preaching and told me it wasn't a good idea to have my girlfriend with me, that it would make it appear I wasn't concentrating fully on my preaching. I didn't want to do anything to detract from the Lord's work."

Ruth's place in his life was becoming clearer and clearer. The never-proposed marriage became a reality August 7, 1939.

Appropriately, the wedding was on a Monday after Willard had closed a meeting the night before at Cane Creek in Marshall County. He and many of the wedding party drove all night to Atlanta, where the wedding was held at the Seminole Church of Christ. "Next time you get married, I want it to be closer to home," homebody Dump Collins joked with his son after the long ride.

Ruth's sister Chick (Mrs. Martha Hammond) was Maid of Honor, while friends Jewell Durdin and Eugenia Hart were in the wedding. Bud Morris served as an usher, and Charles Chumley, who became the long-time minister of the Granny White congregation where the Collinses worship, sang.

Music was provided by Frances Pullias on the organ. Her husband, Athens Clay Pullias, officiated.

The newlyweds headed south, spending their first night in Macon, Georgia, and then going on to Panama City, Florida, and New Orleans. A week later they were back in Marshall County where Willard was preaching a meeting at the Catalpa congregation. Within a month they would begin their first located ministry among the special people at Old Hickory.

The Editor and The Orator had become one.

Willard Collins
Bachelor of Ugliness, 1936

Ruth and Willard Collins:
Wedding Day, August 7, 1939

Chapter Three

The Promotional Preacher

It was a totally new experience for the young preacher and his wife of only two weeks. Heretofore he had preached in monthly appointments and protracted meetings. Now he had a weekly responsibility of preaching, teaching, and encouraging a large church to even greater heights and outreach.

Willard Collins accepted the challenge of the third largest congregation among churches of Christ in Davidson County, Tennessee, when he moved to Old Hickory in August 1939. Willard and Ruth moved into their first home, an apartment in Dupontonia, a small settlement on the outskirts of the Du Pont Company town of Old Hickory. It must have been a frightening prospect for the young couple, but they were young and he was already known for his preaching style—including the booming voice.

Fulltime preachers were rare in Nashville and Middle Tennessee. Only two other churches—Central and Russell Street—completely supported their preachers, E. W. McMillan and S. H. Hall, respectively. In part, this was due to the influences of David Lipscomb, who feared the professional preacher. His reasoning was that a church should do its own work.

The foundation, however, was already in place at Old Hickory. Started in 1920 with only two families, the church functioned without a meetinghouse until 1926. Two years later, the church employed a young man, C. J. Garner, to fill the pulpit. He quickly put everyone to work. By 1930, twelve classrooms were needed. During the next year, the auditorium was enlarged. Not a dynamic pulpit speaker, Garner emphasized church growth through involvement. By 1939, when Garner moved to Union City, Tennessee, the church had 850 members. The Old Hickory Church of Christ was on the verge of its greatest years of activity and service.

The right man was available to help give leadership to this vital church. However, Collins' introduction to Old Hickory was not a red-letter day. E. L. Moore of the Trinity Lane church, one of Willard's monthly appointments, traveled with the young preacher to Old Hickory on the Wednesday evening before Thanksgiving in 1938. He presented a sermon, but all the elders were absent. He had to return later for his "trial" sermon when A. Crawford, S. W. Lawson, Leonard Newsom, and F. W. Jaynes, the elders, were present.

Never before involved in local work, the new preacher built on the methods and accomplishments of C. J. Garner. The *Gospel Messenger*, a mainstay in Garner's work, had to be published each week. This became the responsibility of Ruth, since she had been editor of *The Babbler* at Lipscomb. The church paper kept the church and community informed about the people involved at Old Hickory. It was a news paper—very little instruction. Through the paper the church was challenged to increase its giving, as well as encouraged to attend all activities of the church, especially Sunday school and special weekly classes. Recognition and praise filled the pages for those who had excelled. The paper was a reflection of its editor and the young preacher—totally positive.

Collins quickly became involved with this working church. The fall meeting was an event of October with A. S. Landiss of Chattanooga scheduled to preach. A census was taken in The Village, a name often used instead of Old Hickory. Circulars were prepared. Over 2,000 were distributed. Signs were erected. Goals for attendance were established. On October 15, the last day of the meeting, 600 was the magic number for Sunday school. Following the two-week meeting, thirteen persons had been baptized and a record 654 attended Bible classes on that final Sunday.

Willard Collins' special interests became apparent from the very first: preaching, the Sunday school, and young people. Forrest Wilson, a youngster of eleven at the time, remembers Collins' deep booming preaching voice. He was a tall, good-looking, outgoing, jolly fellow, recalls Wilson. Paul Morrison, a current elder at Old Hickory, states that Collins "could preach in a ten-acre field." Remembering those earlier years, Morrison stated: "[A] few can teach better lessons than Collins can, but none gets them across the way he does."

Characteristic of Collins throughout his life has been his emphasis on goals. This can best be seen at Old Hickory. He credits C. J. Garner for this emphasis that both used so effectively. As had been true with Garner, Collins pushed attendance at all classes and preaching services. Goals were established. "Shade" Lawson, an elder who was in charge of the Sunday school, would announce goals and contests between classes to attain the objectives, including Collins' adult class. Banners were often given for percentage growth, again including the large adult class.

Why such an emphasis on the Sunday school? "The Sunday school," says Collins, "puts life in the congregation." C. J. Garner looked forward to the day when one thousand people would attend Bible classes at Old Hickory. Throughout Collins' tenure the one thousand goal was ever present. The church reached its highest mark of 952 on April 26, 1942 during a meeting led by Hulen Jackson. Collins wrote, "Perhaps no other congregation of the church of Christ in the world had a larger attendance than this Sunday."

Sunday school, however, was not the only time for Bible study. On Tuesday evenings classes were held for all ages, including large classes for men and women. As many as 300 students would attend these classes, with a high of 367 reached on November 17, 1941. When more women than men attended, Collins urged: "Let's go men. The women beat us in attendance last week. . . .That will never do." On Thursday the church had its regular mid-week meeting where classes were again held. At various times during Collins' stay at Old Hickory he would have young peoples' classes on Wednesdays at 6 p.m. and on Sundays at 5:10 p.m. prior to the evening worship. Bible drills with competition between the boys and girls were used on many occasions. Declamation contests encouraged teenage boys to speak; the winners received prizes.

Harold Scott remembers this event as encouraging him to become a speech major at David Lipscomb College. Scott recalls: "The memorized speech was 3 minutes long and before the midweek night audience. We were expected to wear ties, our Sunday best and show what we had learned. Judges were selected and we waited with excitement while they picked the winner." His prize was a trip with the young adults to Mammoth Cave, Kentucky.

Besides Harold Scott, a number of preachers were trained in the

Tuesday night sessions. Joe Sanders, Howard Carter, and John Crosslin were some of the first young men who became preachers. Sanders was somewhat older, already working for Du Pont when Collins encouraged him to preach. The church supported their efforts by providing funds for these men to travel to an adjoining county to fill several pulpits. Sanders quit his job at Dupont and entered David Lipscomb College in September 1941, supported by Old Hickory at $100 per month. Among the younger boys who eventually preached were Joe Gray and Philip Morrison. Gray remembers that he could hardly wait until he was eligible to be a part of the class. It was the "in" thing to do. The formal talks were joint projects of father and son. The father usually wrote the talk given by the son.

Young men were not the only ones who competed. On several occasions, debates were arranged between Old Hickory and Charlotte Avenue, where Athens Clay Pullias preached. On April 25, 1941, Howard Carter and William Lawson affirmed, "Resolved that Private Educational Institutions directed by Faithful Christians are Essential to the Proper Training of Children." Old Hickory won the debate by a 2 to 1 margin of the judges. Joe Sanders and N. P. Hagewood led the Old Hickory contingent to Charlotte Avenue on May 16 to debate "Resolved that the Moving Picture has been a Constructive educational Force." The debaters from Charlotte, Roy Osborne and Jasper Acuff, were victorious on this occasion.

Other activities were included in the weekly paper. Other programs of the church claimed Collins' attention. Increasing the weekly contribution was constantly encouraged in the *Gospel Messenger*. When the Collinses arrived in August 1939, the contribution those first Sundays hovered between $100 and $116. By November, Collins was encouraging a $200-per-week contribution. Gifts to the church increased dramatically from 1938 to 1943.

1938	5,218
1939	6,034
1940	9,773
1941	11,130
1942	13,532
1943	17,216

Already Old Hickory had a zone program, with block leaders, organized during the ministry of C. J. Garner. This program was encouraged and implemented by Willard and Ruth Collins when they announced shortly after their arrival that they planned to visit in every church home by the next spring. They did not accomplish their goal, but evidently made a deep impression on the Old Hickory church and community. The crowds increased so dramatically that an expansion of the building was announced during the spring of 1940. Indicative of the growth were the thirty-two persons baptized between September 1939 and March 31, 1940. By March 1940, the membership had grown from 812 to 925-950, for an increase of over ten percent. Even though economically the times were hard, the church sold 300 bonds to raise the $15,000 needed to increase the size of the auditorium to 850 seats. The construction was finished in time for the October meeting with A. S. Landiss.

Why were Willard Collins and the Old Hickory church so successful in 1939 and 1940? It was a church with a will to work under elders who gave leadership. Publicly, Collins carried out the mandate: "Just make the congregation grow." He centered his emphasis on people, a trait inherited from his father. He filled the *Gospel Messenger* each week with names. Members of the congregation who had special achievements, such as William Lawson's election as class president at Dupont High School, or the record of young men who delivered the *Messenger* each Saturday, were included in the weekly bulletin. All those who made perfect marks on Bible lessons were named each week.

The preacher encouraged various types of involvement among members of the Old Hickory church. Soon after the Collinses arrived in The Village, he planned a trip to Union City, Tennessee to visit C. J. Garner in his new work. Three busloads, including Collins, made the trip on a Saturday morning, ate lunch at the city hall while visiting with the Garners, listened to a sermon by Roy Lanier, and then made the long trip home—all in the same day.

Other tours were planned. In April of 1940, two buses filled with seventy eager travelers visited Chattanooga where A. S. Landiss gave them a guided tour of the city. In May of the same year, 105 persons, this time young people, made a trip to Florence, Alabama, where they visited Wheeler and Wilson dams and the Mars Hill church building. The young people could reserve a seat by depositing five cents, and then paying the rest of the two dollar fare in small amounts. In May 1941, the young people traveled to

Chattanooga where they visited Lookout Mountain. Later the young adults took a trip to Mammoth Cave, Kentucky. Willard Collins planned and made each of these trips.

E. R. Harper of Little Rock, Arkansas conducted a meeting for Old Hickory in October of 1941. A month earlier, Harper had held a meeting for the Waverly, Tennessee church. Evidently Collins thought it would be good for a bus load of Villagers to visit Harper in his meeting. A bus filled with thirty-five men and women made the trip, arriving only five minutes before the service. After visiting with Harper the bus began its return to Old Hickory at 10:30 p.m. The trip was a fun experience with H. A. Moody, Old Hickory's regular song leader, leading songs. He even sang a solo: "Gimme De Leaven's." On the return trip, the conversation centered on baldheaded men, with E. R. Harper as the focal point of attention.

The Collins personality added to the preacher's ability to relate with the people of Old Hickory. These people were, for the most part, first generation town dwellers. Most of them had come from east of Old Hickory on the Cumberland Plateau. Few came from outside Southern Kentucky and Middle Tennessee. Having grown up on a farm himself, Collins found it easy to relate to the people of Old Hickory, whom he described as "working people who loved the church" and who "wanted to convert people." Furthermore, states Collins, the people knew how to work under supervision, since the vast majority worked in Du Pont's cellophane and rayon plants where they worked under foremen and supervisors. They were not middle class people looking for satisfaction in material things.

But there was more to it than the economic and social status of Old Hickorians. Both Willard and Ruth Collins had the desire to work with the people and in turn show deep appreciation for things done for them. Shortly after their arrival in 1939, the congregation showered them with an outpouring of food and other things a young family would need. Soon thereafter the church's fall meeting was held. When it was over, the elders gave them an extra week's salary, plus a five-dollar-per-week raise to thirty-five dollars. The young couple could not say "thank you" enough: "Amid our appreciation and amazement we just pause to say thank you all. We will work harder that we might in a little way deserve this big basketful of good things." At Christmas, the Men's Bible Class gave Collins five volumes of a New Testament commentary. Not to be outdone, the Ladies' Class gave the Collinses a fruit cake: ". . .we have both enjoyed [it] so much and will continue to enjoy [it] for several weeks."

The Collinses had a new 1939 Ford automobile when they arrived in Old Hickory. Edgar Green, a friend in Lewisburg, had put an electric lock gasoline cap on the car for them. During the meeting with A. S. Landiss during October 1939, a young man from Old Hickory stole the car while parked near the building. The police later found the automobile in Smithville, Tennessee, where it had run out of gas. The lock on the cap led to the abandonment of the car. Instead of pressing charges against the young man, Collins showed him kindness. John Crosslin relates how the young man followed him on his paper route while they studied the Bible together. Shortly thereafter, the forgiven thief and his entire family, a total of seven, were baptized. The father preached among smaller congregations in northern Middle Tennessee. This is indicative of the qualities of Willard and Ruth Collins that endeared them to the entire community of Old Hickory.

The Collinses moved to Old Hickory amid hard times of the Depression and the sounds of war in Europe and Asia. The first two years were extraordinary periods of growth, with new records being established only to be broken in a short while. The war in Europe and Asia did not reach Tennessee until December 7, 1941 when the Japanese attacked Pearl Harbor, four days before the birth of the Collins' first child, Carole. On the third Sunday of December, Collins announced that ninety-three Christians had been added to the church since the third Sunday in September. Sixty-six of these had been baptisms. The war, however, quickly made an impact on the Old Hickory Church of Christ.

Soon the young men and women of the congregation were going off to war. Since Du Pont was a large defense contractor, many Old Hickory employees were transferred to other company plants. One result of the transfers was the support of a new congregation in Wilmington, Delaware, the home office of Du Pont. Several were transferred to Martinsville, Virginia. A large contingent went across the country to the Hanford Works centered at Richland, Washington. A number of men left Old Hickory for defense work with other companies. Still others returned to the family farm in what was called "the back-to-the-farm movement." Even though conversions continued at a rather brisk rate, the church lost membership through the duration of the war. Five young men left for the military in one week. During a week in 1943, eight families left for other work.

If the large numbers had not left Old Hickory, the church would easily have reached 1,000 in Sunday school during H. Leo Boles' meeting in October 1943. Instead, only 916 were present. By 1943, Collins counted 151 members who had moved away since 1941. In late 1943, the membership had dropped to 850. Even with this decline, Old Hickory reached its all-time record on October 31, 1943 during the meeting led by I. A. Douthitt. But this record was dulled when sixty-three of the churches' young men and women were away from home in military service.

The war came very close to home when a number of the congregation's young men were killed during the conflict. Among these was Frank Gray, a son of one of the elders, D. C. Gray. The death of his son on foreign soil likely caused Gray to become more interested in foreign missions. Soon after the outbreak of war, forty-seven women met on Wednesday, January 28, 1942, to wrap surgical bandages for the Red Cross. Later they moved the work from the church building to a school next door so more might be involved. Collins wrote of this work: "If our men and boys can give all their time and lives to help win the war, the women and girls should be willing to give a day or at least one-half day each week to this most worthy cause."

Willard Collins was an outstanding local preacher. His personality and work habits were qualities churches look for when desiring a preacher. His sermons covered the special needs of Old Hickory. On other occasions he used doctrinal topics reflecting some of the issues of the day: premillennialism, Bollism, secularism. During much of his time in Old Hickory, he used the *Gospel Advocate Quarterly* for his adult classes. He discovered, however, that a series of lessons on the home attracted large crowds, evidently fulfilling a great need of the people. Early in 1942 he began a series of lessons entitled "A Christian Living in a Government at War."

In the pulpit Willard Collins always felt most at home and most successful. With that first Oklahoma meeting in 1936, Collins knew that his greatest success as a preacher would be as an evangelist in short-term preaching engagements. Each summer Collins spent his time holding meetings in an ever widening circle. The church brought in special preachers, such as Andy T. Richie, Sr., to fill the pulpit during Collins' absence. By September 1942, Collins suggested the possibility of a second man for the church in Old Hickory. Thus one preacher could be present at all times. A second advantage would be the ability to sponsor more mission meetings. A weekly contribution of $300 per week would allow the hiring of the second man.

From 1942 onward, Collins spent more and more time in evangelistic efforts. In 1943 he conducted more than ten meetings, many of them of two-week duration. On November 1, 1943, Collins took Ruth to Madison Hospital where she gave birth to their second daughter, Corinne. Before her birth he fulfilled a speaking engagement at troubled David Lipscomb College's Chapel, learned of the birth of Corinne, and then caught a train for Detroit, Michigan, where he was scheduled for a meeting with the Strathmoor congregation. He saw his daughter for the first time two weeks later.

Old Hickory hired Joe Sanders to return as the second man in June 1943. Sanders did much of the preaching for the remainder of the year. No sooner had Sanders accepted the appointment, however, than he asked to be relieved so that he could accept the pulpit position with the Highland church in Columbia, Tennessee. In the meantime, Old Hickory hired Rufus Clifford to share the work of the congregation. Collins preached during the first three months of 1944 before Clifford arrived in April. For the remainder of the year Collins travelled as an evangelist. In all, he held eighteen meetings with 195 additions, 143 of which were baptisms. He did not preach at Old Hickory for seven months. During the fall of that year, Collins accepted an appointment with David Lipscomb College in its expansion program. He concluded his preaching at Old Hickory with sermons on three Sundays in December.

Evangelism was in Willard Collins' blood. His work at Lipscomb would allow him twelve or thirteen meetings each year. So in December 1944, Willard and Ruth Collins, along with daughters Carole and Corinne, left one of the foremost congregations among churches of Christ. Not until 1947 would Collins again accept the pulpit of a local church, Charlotte Avenue in West Nashville.

* * *

Willard Collins' mentor and friend, Athens Clay Pullias, had been the minister for the Charlotte Avenue church for thirteen years. He began his work there shortly after becoming associated with David Lipscomb College in 1934, the same year that Willard Collins entered Lipscomb as a first year student. Now the student would succeed the teacher as the pulpit minister of one of the three largest churches of Christ in Nashville.

Charlotte Avenue was a congregation already past the half-century mark in 1947. David Lipscomb had preached in the area as early as 1876, but there is little evidence that a church was permanently established until 1889. F. B. Srygley and Granville Lipscomb conducted a tent meeting in West Nashville under the direction of the College Street Church of Christ where David Lipscomb served as an elder. Meeting at first on property owned by others, the church constructed its first building in 1892 on a lot given by a land company.

The church quickly grew. Tearing down the original building, the church invested $26,000 in a new meetinghouse in 1921. Pews for the building were purchased by individual members at ten dollars per seat. The oak pews are still in use on the lower level of the auditorium. While construction was underway, the church worshipped under a tent. In 1926 the men of the church dug out the basement to provide additional classrooms.

Athens Clay Pullias was the first regular preacher employed by the church. During his thirteen-year tenure, Pullias introduced a visitation program, conducted surveys and census programs, and organized a training school for all members of the congregation. The church grew by great strides under the preaching of Pullias. By 1941 there were 1,300 who claimed membership at Charlotte Avenue. The church averaged over 500 in Sunday school during 1939.

Because of added duties as president of David Lipscomb College, Pullias could no longer put the same effort into the congregation's work. Many of the programs declined, including the Sunday school, which dipped to an average of only 301 in 1946. Therefore, he resigned his regular work with the church, but recommended his vice president at Lipscomb, Willard Collins, as the located preacher. Because of Collins' success at Old Hickory, the decision was not difficult. Collins began his work with Charlotte Avenue on January 5, 1947 when 1,100 worshippers crowded into the building.

The Collins touch was quickly evident. At Old Hickory, Collins had learned the importance of the church paper. Therefore, prior to the second Sunday of January, *The Visitor* began publication with Willard Collins as editor. The headline on page one noted the 1,100 in worship, but the numbers in both Sunday school attendance and the contribution were not pleasing to the editor. It bothered him that only 360 attended Bible classes on Sunday and the contribution was only $452.52. Charlotte consistently had worship audiences

numbering 200 larger than Old Hickory, but Sunday school attendance lagged well behind. On March 9, Old Hickory had 713 present for Sunday school. Said Collins: "We have larger audiences
at 11:00 by more than 200, but not at 9:45." Charlotte's goal was
only 400. Ever establishing goals to work toward, the elders
challenged the church in 1948 with the following:

Weekly Contribution	$500
Sunday School	500
Worship	1,015
Training School	200

The months from January to June were important for reaching the
goals. Usually the church pushed to attain the goals by the end
of May before Collins began his meeting schedule.

The West Nashville church was unlike Old Hickory. First,
Charlotte was much more professional and middle class. Its elders,
for the most part, were successful businessmen. J. E. Acuff was
vice president of Life and Casualty Insurance Company and R. I.
Wrather was assistant postmaster. Second, Old Hickory was ideally suited for a zoning program. Collins initiated zoning at Charlotte,
but it never functioned as well as in Old Hickory. Soon after the
Collinses' arrival, seventy-nine individuals were put to work in
zones. There was some difficulty in getting assignments returned
to the office.

On the other hand, the membership of Charlotte Avenue had
much the same emphasis as Old Hickory. Many of the members
were first and second generation urban dwellers, having moved
from the rural areas to the west of Nashville. For the most part,
these people had the same basic commitment to religion as the people of Old Hickory. The greatest need was for someone to channel
the latent energy located in such a large body of people.

That someone was Willard Collins. Goal-setting continued to be
his method. Every week the numbers present in all activities were
given. Goals for the next Sunday or the next training school meeting
were suggested. Beyond the immediate, long-range plans were
made. By April 1947, Collins was urging an attendance of 500 in
Sunday school. On April 27, they reached their goal when 509 were
present. This broke the attendance record for Sunday school at
Charlotte.

Collins believed in competition. He had learned the method well from C. J. Garner. The two men carried on a friendly battle for second place among Nashville churches—Old Hickory was always number one. In March 1950, Garner wrote in his bulletin:

Madison Second Place Again
Madison just barely did squeeze past Charlotte Avenue last Sunday into second place in Davidson County. Old Hickory—684, Madison—487, Charlotte Avenue—483.

During the same period, Collins and Avis Wiggins, the preacher for Lewisburg's Church Street congregation, initiated a friendly contest. During 1947 through 1951, Lewisburg was constantly ahead of Charlotte Avenue, but by 1949 the West Nashville church began averaging 500 in Sunday school. Early in 1953, Charlotte averaged 647.4 persons in Bible classes to Lewisburg's 640.7.

As a result of the efforts of Collins and the members at Charlotte, the Sunday school attendance increased dramatically during Collins' tenure.

1946	301
1947	365
1948	397
1949	470
1950	495
1951	540
1952	611
1953	660
1954	644

On April 26, 1953, Collins noted that Charlotte had 738 in Bible classes. Madison had 709. It was friendly, but the competition stimulated growth in both programs.

Indicative of Collins' emphasis upon enthusiasm to help build a church, the November 10, 1950 *Visitor* noted a number of accomplishments. The contribution was $700 on the previous Sunday. The two previous Sundays saw 581 and 589 attend Sunday school. The audience filled the auditorium, and the large room behind the baptistry overflowed with worshipers. On Wednesday, 100 ladies attended their special class. The Thursday evening training class had attendance on consecutive weeks of 332, 336, and 333. During the previous week, ten new members were added to the congregation through baptism. The enthusiasm generated by goal setting, competition, and challenges was a trademark of Collins' two ministries.

A fourth ingredient Collins incorporated into his work both at Old Hickory and Charlotte Avenue was fellowship. In Old Hickory, he encouraged bus trips to places of interest. At Charlotte, he emphasized picnics and parties for his auditorium class of young married people. After a while the class sponsored a special activity each quarter. The men of the congregation began meeting occasionally for a meal at Sloan Hall across from the church building at 46th and Charlotte. Collins suggested that such meetings were good so that the men might get to know each other better.

Evidently his methods for the class worked. He began the class with only seventy-six members in 1947. By March he had an all-time high to date of eighty-seven. His new goal was 106. On May 3, 1953 when 985 attended Sunday school at Charlotte Avenue, 423 persons attended Willard Collins' class.

A fifth strength Collins brought to local work was a strong pulpit presence. With his booming voice he quickly gained the attention of his auditors. Chester Jaynes, an elder appointed during Collins' tenure, suggests that he accomplished his greatest work in the pulpit. He further describes Collins' style as a strong, deliberate speaker who never high-pressures or browbeats anyone into responding; his concern for the welfare of everyone becomes evident rather quickly to all who hear him. Chester Jaynes can appreciate his description of Collins because he was one of the first persons baptized under Collins' preaching at Charlotte in February 1947.

To deal with the increased numbers attending Charlotte Avenue, the elders in 1951 initiated a building plan to make the auditorium the largest among churches of Christ east of the Mississippi River. The seating capacity of the auditorium before remodeling was only 750. Chairs were placed in every aisle and classrooms had to be opened to accommodate the crowds; with the new facility an audience of 1,515 could be seated without extra chairs. To accommodate the increased size, a complete balcony was constructed. With increased space on the main level, the building could hold the larger crowds. Besides the auditorium, eight classrooms were added. They added a sound-proof chapel that could also serve as a radio broadcast studio.

The new facilities were formally opened on June 22, 1952, when Carroll Ellis began a meeting. All former members were encouraged to participate in Homecoming. In an attempt to have 1,000 in Sunday school, 300 persons made 1,500 calls inviting guests to the big day. The elders planned for the contribution to pay for the new seats needed for the addition. The figures for the day were impressive: 821 in Sunday school, 1,547 for worship (32 chairs were placed in the aisles), and a contribution of $2,521.76. This sixty-year old congregation had renewed vigor under the dynamic preaching of G. Willard Collins.

With the end of World War II, there was a pent-up desire to preach the gospel to the former enemy. Quickly, Charlotte Avenue became involved. The church early supported Delmar Bunn, an American, in Germany. When a number of German young men came to David Lipscomb College for education, Charlotte Avenue took Dieter Alten as its very own. When he returned to his homeland, the West Nashville church supported him in his work. Besides the German work, Charlotte supported a number of mission efforts in foreign countries and in the United States. Of the total contributions for 1950-51-52 of $114,818.61, the church spent forty-five percent, or $51,963.84, on mission work. When Otis Gatewood came to the States in 1950, he gave a special report at the Charlotte Avenue building on New Year's Eve. The church collected an additional contribution of $1,738.04. Additionally, men of the Charlotte Avenue church oversaw a fund to support foreign students at Lipscomb.

In 1950, the church began a weekly radio program over WNAH. Within two years the programs from Charlotte were being broadcast over six stations—four in Virginia, one in Kentucky, and one in Nashville. When the new construction was contemplated in 1951, the chapel included a radio studio. Local people were involved, including Brown Vandiver leading the singing, Sidney Hooper announcing, and Willard Collins and others doing the speaking.

The Visitor did not record the total number of baptisms each year while Collins filled the pulpit at Charlotte. Typical of his ministry were the reports of two periods in 1947 and 1948. From January through May 1947, eighteen persons were baptized. During April and May 1948, thirty-one additions were recorded, seventeen of which were baptisms. During Batsell Barrett Baxter's meeting in October 1947, fourteen persons submitted to baptism. Two years later, following a trip to Europe, Baxter returned to Charlotte for a meeting with fifteen baptisms. These were included in the total of forty-nine baptisms between September 1948 and November

1949. During the early fifties, rarely did a Sunday pass without some response. Collins, in his personal records, listed 381 baptisms while at Charlotte.

Athens Clay Pullias had initiated a training program at Charlotte Avenue while he served the church. In fact, he was the preacher when Old Hickory debated young men from Charlotte. Collins continued the training class methods at Charlotte, where he worked with young men in the sixth, seventh, and eighth grades. Several young men, including James Vandiver, committed themselves to preaching after having been in the class.

Toward the end of 1953, Collins told the elders that he had become so involved with his duties at Lipscomb that he could no longer continue at Charlotte Avenue. Early in 1954 the elders announced that Mack Craig, principal of David Lipscomb High School, would succeed Collins on January 1, 1955. Collins continued his work on through 1954, but not with the success he had enjoyed previously. Attendance lagged slightly, only to improve again within two years. But it had been a good seven years. Collins had shared with the church his goals, enthusiasm, and public relations while teaching both from the pulpit and in the classroom. It was a work well done.

* * *

How does one assess Willard Collins as a local preacher? An assessment of the times in which he served the two churches makes it much easier to understand his success. It was a time when religion was a part of most Americans' lives. "Church going" was the thing to do. Collins' promotional approach to church growth was easy because he had a good product to sell. He was the master promoter. He had enthusiasm. He was convinced that his was the most important work in the world. Shortly after he arrived at Charlotte Avenue, he wrote: "Millions are lost. They need the Gospel. May all of us do our part." The work and the man were joined at Old Hickory and Charlotte Avenue.

Chapter Four

Harvest Time for Souls

Barton Stone, early nineteenth-century Restorer, called them revivals. Alexander Campbell did not like the word "revival," so he introduced into the Restoration Movement the concept of the protracted meeting. At some time late in the nineteenth century or early in the twentieth, the idea of the gospel meeting was introduced among churches of Christ.

Willard Collins numbers among the most successful evangelists of the past fifty years. Collins has preached thousands of sermons, with the vast majority delivered during special meetings denoted by the term "Gospel Meeting." From the day he baptized his first convert in Orlando, Florida, during the summer of 1935, until December 1984, over 12,000 persons responded to Collins' preaching. Of this total, 6,859 were baptized.

Because of his popularity over such an expanse of time, Willard Collins must rank near the top among evangelists in churches of Christ. During the last years of the nineteenth century, James A. Harding and T. B. Larimore were the most sought-after evangelists. In the twentieth century, N. B. Hardeman, Foy E. Wallace, Jr., and G. C. Brewer were in constant demand. Since the late 1930s, Collins has had to refuse more meetings than he has accepted. Most churches ask him to return for a later series, oftentimes finding it necessary to project ten years into the future. In addition to the local congregational meetings, he was in great demand for cooperative campaigns during the 1960s when they were popular.

Why has he remained in such demand for fifty years? Frank

Pack, a professor at Pepperdine University and a fellow student with Collins at Vanderbilt University, describes him even as a young man:

> He was always an impressive speaker. He had a very commanding voice....He had a special gift in being able to move people to obey the gospel. His style of preaching was simple, but his person was impressive and his sermons carried conviction....He is very unassuming.
>
> In my day of young preachers, it was popular for a preacher to use many scriptures. Willard did not do that very much. But he was a master of illustrations for his points. He knew how to drive them home with conviction that moved people.

Even though Willard Collins was successful as a located preacher, his training and personal qualities were especially suited for evangelistic outreach. "A gospel meeting," said Collins, "is a harvest time for souls."

* * *

As true of most young men, Willard Collins did not begin as a sought-after evangelist. Between his first two years of college, he baptized six in Orlando, Florida. Before his 1935 year at Lipscomb he returned to Lewisburg where he baptized five, one of whom was his father.

His first evangelistic effort was in Prairie Hill, near Duncan, Oklahoma, in 1936. The crowds and the results foreshadowed the future success of the young preacher. Mrs. Ike Pollack recalls that first meeting: "We [Prairie Hill church] had a membership of probably 60 to 70, but we had large crowds at his meetings. People came for miles. We probably had 200-300 or maybe more to attend." Concerning his preaching style, Mrs. Pollack remembers: "He was such a dynamic speaker he could hold their attention. His lessons were so simple and clear anyone could understand what to do to become a Christian." Because the crowds were so large, Collins stood on the front steps of the building while his listeners gathered in the yard where they sat on improvised benches. Electric lights, which attracted many distracting bugs, were strung across the crowded church lawn. Since the building did not have a baptistry, the fifteen persons who responded were immersed in a farm pond after changing their clothing "in the bushes behind the dam."

Why was Willard Collins so successful at Prairie Hill during his meetings of 1936, 1937, 1938, and 1941? Mrs. Pollack believes it was because of "his Christ-like life" and 'his lessons were on a level that anyone could understand. He didn't use a lot of big, hard to understand words." Collins knew how to work with people: "He visited in the homes of everyone. He could converse with people from every walk of life."

Collins, however, was not yet a well-known evangelist in his home region. In 1937, H. Leo Boles urged forty-five churches of Christ in Nashville to have simultaneous meetings the following year. His target was not reached, but nineteen churches scheduled meetings for the end of April 1938. Boles preached for the Chapel Avenue church, Ira Douthitt was the speaker at Grace Avenue, Lischey Avenue engaged E. W. McMillan, and E. R. Harper preached for Boles' home church, Twelfth Avenue, North. A young boy preacher, Willard Collins, was the speaker for Eleventh Street.

The Eleventh Street meeting raised eyebrows around Nashville. The nineteen churches attracted a combined audience of nearly 100,000 with a daily average attendance of 6,002. As a result of these efforts, 330 persons were baptized and ninety-one were restored. Willard Collins' meeting attracted an average attendance of 331 with fifty-four baptisms and thirteen restorations. Only Grace Avenue with an average of 701 per night had a greater response: sixty-two baptisms and ten restorations. The name Willard Collins became recognized throughout Nashville and Middle Tennessee.

Collins continued his education at Vanderbilt University through June 1939. He found time, nevertheless, to preach in a number of gospel meetings, including a return to Eleventh Street. Premillennialism was a current topic in Nashville. At the same time Collins was at Eleventh Street, Foy E. Wallace, Jr., was just a few blocks away at Chapel Avenue. On two Sunday afternoons Wallace spoke at the Dixie Tabernacle on issues facing churches of Christ. Most preachers in Nashville attended, but Collins did not attend; in fact, he does not recall the huge rallies. This is somewhat amazing since Collins gives Wallace credit for encouraging him to preach. Incidentally, his second meeting was not as impressive as the one in 1938. Only eight were baptized. As has been true of much of Collins' preaching, Eleventh Street invited him back for meetings in 1963, 1968, 1973, 1976, and 1980.

The last year of the 1930s was an eventful one for Willard Collins. He finished his graduate program at Vanderbilt, spent a summer holding meetings, married Ruth Morris, and accepted his first local work at Old Hickory. He also reached a milestone, as a hundred persons were baptized in his meetings and at Old Hickory during the year. Not until 1947 would the total fall below the century mark.

Accepting a local pulpit did not diminish Collins' interest in evangelism. He had an agreement with Old Hickory's elders that allowed him to hold meetings during June, July, and August. Since most meetings were of two weeks' duration, his schedule included only six to eight special sessions each year.

Old Hickory helped Collins become involved in evangelism. Members of the congregation had moved to the community from many smaller towns throughout Middle Tennessee and Southern Kentucky. As a result of new friendships, the young Old Hickory preacher began receiving invitations from throughout the region. The Collinses developed many important friendships through their meeting work. One such relationship blossomed with the Hulen Jacksons. During the summer of 1940, Collins preached a series of sermons for the East Side church in Shawnee. Even though it was not where Hulen Jackson preached, the two men met for the first time. In the spring of 1942, the Jacksons came to Tennessee when he held a meeting for the Old Hickory church. Ruth Collins opened her home to the Jacksons, where she introduced them to hot doughnuts and ice cream. The meeting resulted in twenty-six baptisms and four restorations.

In later years, Jackson returned to Nashville for meetings, one of which was with Charlotte Avenue while Collins was the preacher. On several occasions Collins preached in meetings for the Trinity Heights church in Dallas where Jackson was the minister. Ruth always made this trip with her husband to visit friends made in the early 1940s.

On several occasions while at Old Hickory, Collins engaged in gospel meetings in the Nashville area while continuing his work at home. One such series was with the Lischey Avenue church in April and May 1941. Lasting two weeks, the series established church attendance records. When the meeting concluded, thirty-one had been baptized. Indicative of the sermons Collins preached are the following:

Two Things We Must Face.
Man's Most Valuable Possession.
Man's Road Map to Heaven.
Jesus the Savior.
The Holy Spirit in Conversion.
The Church Over Which Christ is Head.
The Church of Christ is Not the
Campbellite Church.

A preaching pattern followed for forty years was established.

Among the most important influences on Willard Collins was E. R. Harper, an outstanding evangelist of the 1930s and the 1940s. During the fall of 1941, Harper returned to Old Hickory for a meeting. Joe Sanders, present for the meeting, remembers Harper as a dynamic speaker whose sermons were simple. He had the ability to move people. Collins gives Harper credit for influencing him to become more involved in evangelism. Harper used prepared charts in his preaching. Shortly thereafter, Collins began chart preaching. Later "Pem" Pemberton of Maryville, Tennessee became Collins' chart illustrator.

On December 7, 1941, the United States was plunged into World War II when Japan bombed Pearl Harbor. Shortly thereafter, thousands of American young men and young women were torn from their homes to travel to foreign lands in defense of their country. At about the same time, Collins decided to give more of his time in evangelistic efforts away from home. He reasoned: If young men can give up their homes to defend the country, surely I can leave home to preach the gospel of Christ.

By early May 1943, Collins began meetings that would keep him away from Old Hickory for the next four months. His travels in 1943 carried him to Shawnee, Oklahoma, Detroit, Michigan, and Springfield, Missouri. The following year his evangelistic efforts were even greater. When Rufus Clifford arrived to fill Old Hickory's pulpit in April 1944, Collins spent his time in revivals until December. He returned to the pulpit of Old Hickory for only three Sundays before leaving to accept a position at David Lipscomb College.

It was from a September meeting being conducted in Sparta, Tennessee, that Athens Clay Pullias called Collins to Nashville to offer him the position of Associate Director of the Lipscomb Expansion Program. Announcing his decision to the Old Hickory church, Collins wrote:

> Next year I plan to conduct 12 meetings. Some are for
> two Sundays, some for three, and one for four Sundays. This
> means a lot of preaching and does not leave much time for
> local work.
> I believe my future plans will enable me to make known
> the gospel of Christ to more people than ever before.

Reporting his work for 1944 in the *Gospel Messenger*, Collins re-
counted eighteen meetings held during the year, beginning on
March 27 and ending on November 16. From Nashville he travelled
south to Tampa, Florida, east to Wilmington, Delaware (a mission
point of the Old Hickory church), and west to Abilene, Texas. The
meetings resulted in 149 baptisms and forty restorations. But the
war influenced attendance and results. Said Collins:

> War conditions have hurt attendance in cities but atten-
> dance in smaller towns is practically normal as far as my
> meetings were concerned. In several places attendance once
> or twice was larger than even before the war. It is com-
> mon consent over the country that the lost are not being
> reached in Gospel Meetings now as in former years.

* * *

The new year of 1945 afforded great challenges for the young
man of thirty years. He became totally involved in raising funds
to make Lipscomb a senior college. He held meetings across the
country, returning in March to his first summer's work at Orlando, Florida for a four-Sunday engagement. During the year, 124
responded for baptism. In 1946, the response included 130 baptisms and thirty-four restorations.

Along with his evangelistic outreach, Collins returned to local
work at Charlotte Avenue in 1947. His number of meetings declined
as did the total responses. Both 1947 and 1948 were below average
years with eighty-three and seventy-six baptisms respectively. But
1949 saw a total reversal. Returning to Old Hickory for a meeting,
Collins had the greatest response in crowds and baptisms ever in
his preaching experience. When the last day's service concluded,
111 persons had been baptized and fifty-five had been restored.
Collins proved that it is possible to go home again. He conducted

four other meetings at Old Hickory—1953, 1964, 1970, and 1974. The five meetings resulted in 199 baptisms and ninety-nine restorations.

Collins began his career holding gospel meetings in Marshall County. In 1950, he returned to his home congregation for a series of sermons. Remembered well by his hometown, native son Willard Collins was welcomed by a record Sunday school crowd of 1,005. An audience of 1,500 heard Collins' sermons and four responded for baptism. The second Sunday's crowds were even larger—1,054 for Bible classes and 1,700 to 1,800 for the preaching service. A total of sixty persons responded to the invitation, fifty-one for baptism. Avis Wiggins, the local preacher, announced that the crowds were the largest in the church's history.

With the exception of his Far East tour in 1961, Collins' automobile trip with his family to Richland, Washington was his longest journey for preaching. Richland is the residential city for the Hanford Engineering Works where the ingredients of the atomic bomb were developed during World War II. Many employees of Du Pont were transferred from Old Hickory to Richland in 1944. As a result, a church began in that new town. Two of the elders appointed by the church were among the transferees—E. L. Kelly and Buford W. Hooper.

The Collinses made the trip in a new Studebaker automobile in 1953. They placed a mattress between the seats of the car so the girls could sleep. Meals were often cooked along the highways. It was an experience that all the Collinses recall. It was, nevertheless, a successful trip as nineteen responded to his preaching—seven baptisms and twelve restorations. The same year saw 183 baptisms and seventy-one restorations.

Willard Collins concluded his local preaching with the Charlotte Avenue church in December 1954. His duties at school would not allow him sufficient time to carry on the work of a large church. Since 1954, the entirety of his preaching has been by appointment, including Sundays, week-long meetings, and special campaigns.

* * *

In 1955, Willard Collins reached his fortieth birthday. No longer was he the young boy preacher. Now he was in demand for special kinds of preaching endeavors, especially campaigns, which became a newer method of evangelism in the 1960s.

The city-wide campaign was not new in the 1960s. Clearly the outstanding example in this regard had been the Hardeman Tabernacle Sermons in Nashville beginning in 1922. All together there had been five evangelistic efforts with the last one in 1941. Foy Wallace was the speaker in the Music Hall meetings in Houston in 1945. Reuel Lemmons, commenting on the importance of area-wide campaigns, remarked:

> Without exception we feel that they are outstanding demonstrations of the church's strength and unity. Nothing speaks any more loudly than such a demonstration....[T]hey are an attempt to reach out and affect numbers of people who are not reached by the regular meetings held by the congregations.

Willard Collins was the most frequently called person when a campaign was contemplated. The reason can be seen in the results of his meetings between 1955 and 1963:

Year	Meetings Held	Baptisms	Restorations	Number Placing Membership	Total Responses	Average per Meeting
1955	15	199	117	9	325	21+
1956	14	131	37	2	170	14+
1957	14	134	150	13	297	21
1958	15	179	35	19	233	15+
1959	13	194	113	33	340	26
1960	17	281	150	33	464	27+
1961	14	248	115	17	380	27
1962	18	170	101	53	324	18
1963	19	251	291	5	547	28+
9 Year Total:	139	1,787	1,109	184	3,080	22

Collins' long-time associate, Athens Clay Pullias, summed up the qualities that have made him a successful evangelist:

> Brother Collins' outstanding success as a gospel preacher witnesses that the word of God is still "quick and powerful." He proclaims God's word in all of its purity, and he preaches it from the heart. The combination of a powerful voice, a sincere appeal, and a personality that radiates love

for his fellow man has made him one of the most powerful gospel preachers of our day.

Willard Collins was not the evangelist in the first campaigns during the middle of the 1950s. His very close friend, Batsell Barrett
Baxter, was the speaker in a special effort in Lubbock, Texas. In
1956, the Broadway church, with help from other local churches,
sponsored Baxter in a 3,500-seat auditorium in the Pan Handle city.
Two years later, Baxter was the speaker for a similar effort in San
Angelo, Texas.

Interest aroused by these successful campaigns caused churches
of Christ in the Wichita Falls, Texas, area to dream of a similar
meeting in their city. Plans were laid as early as 1959, but the campaign did not happen until 1960. Twelve churches cooperated in
the effort. To let the community know about the meetings, the churches spent $6,275 on advertising. A "kickoff" dinner was scheduled
for January 25, 1960 at Midwestern University, where the 600 in
attendance heard Willard Collins. He flew in especially for the
gathering.

For eight nights beginning February 14, Collins spoke to thousands
of people on the theme "A Plea For Christ." As usual, the response
to his preaching was excellent with thirty-two baptisms and seventy-
two restorations. The grand total for attendance was 22,000 persons. Congregational singing was led by Richard Daughtry. The sermons were published under the title *A Plea For Christ*.

The Collins-Craig Auditorium Meeting of October 1962 had to
be a climax in the preaching career of Willard Collins. Even though
he had been successful—places far from Tennessee, his greatest
triumphs had been "back home" in Old Hickory and Lewisburg.
Now he had the opportunity to preach to the entire community
of Nashville as the city opened its new $5,000,000 Municipal
Auditorium. It would be the fulfillment of any preacher's dream.

The elders at Charlotte Avenue, friends of long-standing, sponsored the meeting with the help of sister congregations throughout
the area. Chosen by the elders to chair the meeting was Athens
Clay Pullias, president of Lipscomb and former preacher for the
Charlotte Avenue church. On January 28, 1962, the following announcement was made to the membership of the Charlotte Avenue
church:

The Charlotte Avenue congregation has been given the opportunity to hold a gospel meeting in Nashville's new Municipal Auditorium October, 7-14, 1962. The elders felt that this was an unprecedented opportunity to advance the Kingdom of God and therefore accepted this great responsibility. After prayerful reflection, Brother Willard Collins has been chosen to do the preaching and Brother Mack Wayne Craig selected to lead the singing. It is our judgment that these two men are ideally suited to make this meeting a historic step forward in the work of spreading New Testament Christianity.

Shortly thereafter, elaborate plans were underway to fill every seat in the new facility. Carl McKelvey and Winston Tynes were charged with the responsibility of getting 10,000 persons for each service and a total attendance of 83,200. All together ninety-two congregations cooperated in providing funds and the three hundred fifty to four hundred ushers needed for each night.

The attendance was beyond every expectation. Additional seats were brought in when it was realized that the crowds would more than fill the auditorium. On the first Sunday night the audience reached 15,000—with 13,000 in the auditorium and 2,500 in the corridors. From 5,000 to 8,000 persons were turned away. Those who were able to gain admittance heard Collins speak on "Trusting Faith in God: The Need of This Hour." For the remainder of the meeting, Collins used subjects and themes thousands of people had already heard and topics he has used to reach thousands since 1962. His closing presentation was a traditional Collins sermon, "Going Home."

With the closing service on October 14, the Collins-Craig Auditorium Meeting was pronounced an overwhelming success. The total attendance was 90,467, an average of 11,308 each evening. Nothing of the sensational surrounded the meeting. Clay Pullias remarked:

The meeting was planned, advertised and held in the spirit of a prayer meeting. It was not a pep rally and was not treated as such. The sensational in any form was strictly avoided: Multiple invitation hymns were not sung. Because of the nature and plan of the meetings, only sixteen were baptized and fifteen were restored.

Invitations for area-wide meetings, campaigns, and other special efforts quickly found their way to Nashville. Moving west of the Mississippi River, Collins conducted a campaign in Shreveport, Louisiana, between April 14-21, 1963. Participants came from Texas and Arkansas to hear the Tennessee evangelist. On the last night of the meeting forty-five persons responded to the invitation, twenty-eight of whom were baptized. In recalling his meetings, the last night in Shreveport remains vivid in Collins' mind. Reporting the campaign, Ira North urged: "If you are fortunate enough to have Willard Collins scheduled for a meeting, why not consider turning it into a city-wide or area-wide meeting?"

Collins' next stop was Fort Worth where he spoke on the 1963 Fort Worth Bible Forum. Beginning on June 9, the evangelist spoke to crowds of 9,000, 6,000, 6,000, and 8,000. Using the theme "Let Us Go Back to the Bible for Authority in Religion," Collins impressed Thomas Warren, who wrote:

> The preaching of Willard Collins was both true to God's word and was powerfully delivered. It was the kind of preaching which both makes and leaves a deep impression on the hearts of those who heard.

Over the next several years, Collins would serve as the evangelist in a dozen or more campaigns. In 1963, he remained in Texas for campaigns in Waco and Brownfield. The following year, Lipscomb's vice president was involved in two campaigns that continue to stand out in his mind. He went all the way to San Francisco, California, to hold a five-night, area-wide meeting. Evidently because of Lipscomb's racial stance at the time, black preachers boycotted the sessions. Some two hundred to two hundred fifty persons refused to attend the meeting because of the boycott. This had never happened at one of Collins' meetings.

In July 1964, Collins had an unusual experience in St. Louis. He participated in his first televised area-wide meeting. For five nights the evangelist spoke in the Knorazann Room of the Chase Park Plaza Hotel. Led by the Wood River, Illinois church, thirty congregations cooperated to fill the hall each evening and to finance the telecast. The television station, KPLR, estimated the audience at two and a half million.

Ruth Collins returned home to Atlanta with her evangelist husband in 1965 for a campaign held in the city's municipal auditorium.

L. O. Sanderson—well-known songleader, editor of hymnals, and author of hymns— directed the worship in song. At the time there were only 4,588 members of churches of Christ in Atlanta in eighteen congregaitons. Through the dynamic preaching of Collins, twenty-five persons were baptized. An additional forty-three were restored. The authorities for the auditorium reported that the crowds, averaging 4,800 per night, were the largest to attend religious services in the facility.

Evidently the Collins' appeal reached beyond the Southeast and Texas. In 1967, he traveled to Albuquerque, New Mexico, for a five-night, area-wide meeting under the general oversight of the Candelavia Church of Christ. His sermon selection was typical of Willard Collins:

A Plea For Christ from Behind the Cross
The Most Sobering Fact About Sin
What Jesus Can Mean to You
The Power of the Resurrection Gospel
The Reality of the Judgment and Eternity

Held at the city's municipal auditorium, the meeting saw thirty-eight respond for baptism and fifty-one restored. A successful meeting, indeed!

Many other campaigns were held between 1955 and 1972, but space will not allow discussion. One preaching trip Collins took, however, must be mentioned. Beginning in 1955, the Far Eastern Fellowship Meeting invited a preacher from the United States to lead military personnel who were members of churches of Christ in a series of special religious services. Those who preceded Collins to Japan were J. D. Bales, H. A. Dixon, Batsell Barrett Baxter, J. D. Thomas, M. Norvel Young, and George S. Benson. Traveling to the Far East in November, Willard and Ruth Collins visited South Korea (where A. R. Holton was serving as a missionary), Hong Kong, Formosa (now Taiwan, where Enoch Thweatt—former Lipscomb student and teacher—was a missionary), the Philippines, and Hawaii. It was an experience not soon forgotten.

* * *

American religion reflected much of what was happening in the broad culture during the last years of the 1960s and the first years of the 1970s. Society was becoming more secular—the religious revival of the 1950s had run its course. Viet Nam shattered the unity of America. College campuses became the scene of demonstrations—the young were alienated from their elders. Racial tensions grew, culminating in the assassination of Martin Luther King, Jr. in 1968.

Churches of Christ were not immune from these destructive symptoms. The growth that had been so obvious in the 1950s and the early 1960s began to slacken after 1965. By the early 1970s many churches were beginning to ask questions about the lack of growth, especially the seeming inability to reach the unconverted. Willard Collins began noticing a major change early in the 1970s. His observations confirm Flavil Yeakley's conclusions about churches of Christ. Indicative of this concern was J. D. Thomas' book *What Lack We Yet?*, published in 1974. Included were numerous essays directed toward what Batsell Barrett Baxter called "The Crisis" in a lecture at Abilene Christian during the lectureship of 1976.

The following figures from Collins' record books indicate the reason for the concern he has voiced since 1973.

Year	Bap- tisms	Restor- ations
1965	244	526
1966	216	242
1967	232	399
1968	209	220
1969	230	238
1970	274	211
1971	220	309
1972	175	338
1973	83	185
1974	120	172
1975	121	161
1976	90	111

The decline began in 1972, but was not particularly obvious until 1973. When Collins accepted the presidency of Lipscomb in 1977 he canceled many of his meetings. He believed his place was on campus.

Even with reduced meetings, the response decline remains rather obvious, reflecting the reduction in outreach noticed by others in churches of Christ. Notice the following:

Year	Bap- tisms	Restor- ations
1977	38	101
1978	46	122
1979	16	68
1980	29	65
1981	20	79
1982	21	36
1983	17	52
1984	8	29

Concerning the recent past, Collins only shakes his head. The crowds have been much smaller than in the 1950s and the 1960s. Few who are not affiliated with churches of Christ have been present in the meetings. Communities where he has visited since the middle 1970s are more interested in other things—youth sports, television, recreation. Maybe, he muses, the times are too prosperous.

* * *

Why has Willard Collins been such a success as an evangelist for fifty years? Why have churches such as Bremen, Georgia, Broadway in Lubbock, Texas, West End in Birmingham, Alabama, Jefferson Street in Orlando, Florida, Milan, Tennessee, and Eleventh Street in Nashville called him back year after year? Why have college churches in Abilene, Texas, Henderson, Tennessee, and Nashville used him time after time? Why was he in such great demand for area-wide meetings when they were so popular in the 1960s?

Always mentioned by observers is Willard Collins' sincerity. He is believable. Joe Sanders, his long-time friend and associate, emphasizes Collins' strong convictions. When he preaches, states Sanders, he leaves his auditors with the conclusion: "This is it!" If Collins believes so strongly what he preaches, then it must be so.

Hulen Jackson recalls his impressions of Collins: "Like a wasp Willard was full grown at the beginning as a preacher. [He is] blessed with a marvelous voice and the ability to think clearly and to express his thoughts with persuasive simplicity." Without exception those asked to evaluate Collins' success as a preacher meniton simplicity. His sermons have always been simple, easily understood by his listeners.

In the same vein, John H. Banister describes Collins in his earlier years as "a dynamic young man, with a lot of enthusiasm, and a tender and persuasive appeal to the unsaved. He had the unique ability to stir, motivate, and move people to accept Christ. This, in my judgment, has been perhaps his greatest strength as a preacher through the years."

Banister recalls a meeting Collins held for the Skilman Avenue church in Dallas during the 1960s. Collins spoke on both radio and television programs, taught Bible classes both for Sunday mornings and evenings, preached three sermons each day, and conducted a young peoples' class prior to the evening services. He preached Monday through Saturday for an early morning meeting for business people. Another morning service was conducted each day at 11 a.m. On Tuesday, Collins spoke at a dinner attended by 400 women.

On the last night, Collins announced that the sermon he had just preached was the forty-second speech he had delivered in Dallas during the eight-day meeting. Banister suggests from this another Collins' strength: "He worked hard, but never complained. This is in vivid contrast to some preachers who come for meetings and complain because we have one week-day service."

A former student at Lipscomb, Mitchell Embry, recalls a Collins meeting at the College church in Abilene. He writes:

> Brother Collins' simple three-point sermon outlines, preached in the love and power of the Spirit of Christ, influenced my preaching and teaching over the years. One such lesson presentation has remained with me. It was during a daily chapel period that brother Collins presented the sermon "God's Time Table," and used his wristwatch (which he usually held in the palm of his hand when teaching or making announcements) to make the points of that sermon.

Embry also states:

> He influenced me by the erect way he stood, the way he dressed, the way he presented the material, the way he befriended each student, and by remaining humble in his high position of service.

At Abilene, Embry, his wife, and two small children lived in an old army barracks. During Collins' meeting for the College church, he, along with local preacher George Bailey, visited in Embry's home. The former Lipscomb student remembers that visit:

> In the midst of his many appointments and dozens of invitations to eat meals in fine furnished homes and restaurants, he and George Bailey came to our small two-room plus kitchen apartment to eat a meal around a 3'x4' rickety table on folding chairs. I remember his warm expression of gratitude and appreciation for our hospitality toward him. Many in his position and with a full schedule would not have had the time to spend with a former student; but, brother Collins takes the time to share himself. That is being godly and that makes him great among men.

Many recall Collins' ability to be "at home" with everyone. This has been a strength of Willard Collins for fifty years. The sermons preached by Collins have not changed dramatically over the years. In fact, some of the sermons he used in the late 1950s remain standard in the 1980s. He has had and continues to have the unique ability to take the same sermon and adapt it to a particular situation. The topics and basic outlines might be the same, but the auditors feel that it is a sermon prepared especially for them.

A typical meeting, whether in the 1960s or the 1980s would include the following themes:

1. Living for Christ
2. Eternity
3. Judgment
4. Making a choice
5. Second coming
6. A lesson on the family
7. The church
8. Sin
9. Submission to God

Beginning in 1963, the most preached sermons would include the following themes:
(The figures on the right indicate how many times each theme appeared as the most preached or the second most preached sermon for

the years 1965 to 1984.)

	First	Second
1. If I Be Lifted Up	1	0
2. Eternity	6	3
3. Judgment	6	3
4. Sin	1	1
5. Living for Christ	2	2
6. Without Christ	2	0
7. Submission	1	4
8. Second Coming	2	0
9. Love	1	2

Each meeting would include a lesson to the family and a special Bible school session with the young people.

His topics for the area-wide meeting in Tupelo, Mississippi, during August of 1964 serve as an excellent example of how he adapted his sermons to special occasions.

1. Let Us Go Back to the Bible
2. To Find Two Ways and Two Destinies
3. To Find Christ as Our Example in Submission to God
4. To Find the Gospel—Christ's Message of Salvation
5. To Find the Church For Which Christ Died
6. To Find God's Pattern For the Family
7. For God's Picture of the Vastness of Eternity

These sermons are likely recognized by those who have listened to Collins during the last several decades.

Occasionally the sermons were varied. When he conducted an area-wide meeting in Wichita, Kansas during 1976, the churches chose as a theme: Jesus Now. The topics were somewhat unusual for a Collins' meeting, but they were used occasionally in later meetings. On the other hand, it is possible to note his constant themes in the six sermons preached.

1. He Lives
2. He Loves
3. He Cares
4. He Saves
5. He Intercedes
6. He Leads

In 1973, Collins was the featured speaker for the Yosemite Family Encampment. The themes discussed were some of his favorites—sermons he has used to move people to respond for years.

1. It is Great to be a Christian
2. I Love the Church
3. Judgment Day is Real
4. When Obedience to God is turned into Permissiveness

On Monday and Tuesday, he spoke to the young people on these themes:

1. Decisions Determine Destinies
2. It is Foolish Not to Be a Christian

Evidently the emphasis made on the love of the church during the 1970s was a response to much of the negative attitude toward the church at that time.

The key to understanding Willard Collins as an evangelist is his interest and concern for people. When he preaches, his audience knows he is interested in them individually—he wants all of them to be saved; it would hurt him personally if any were lost. In whatever he does as an evangelist, he is a people person.

* * *

For fifty years Collins has traveled across the United States preaching the gospel of Christ. He has baptized literally thousands of persons. Through 1984, 6,859 had been baptized during his meetings. The grand total of baptisms and restorations is 12,485. Truly, Willard Collins has been the outstanding evangelist among churches of Christ since the 1940s. It all began nearly fifty years ago at Prairie Hill, Oklahoma. He has been a man for his times.

Collins-Craig Auditorium Meeting, 1962

Chapter Five

The Preaching
Vice President

As Americans fought for their lives and for the country they loved on foreign soil in the early forties, David Lipscomb College was being torn by theological and philosophical differences that could have left the small junior college devastated.

By late 1943, President E. H. Ijams, several faculty members, and some veteran board members had resigned in the wake of controversies dealing with premillennialism and the more vague "Bollism." Various factions were striving for control of the school, and a number of candidates were emerging for leadership roles.

The college's board of directors turned to a pair of able young men—two of the best preachers in the brotherhood, whose love affair with David Lipscomb College was well known—to carry out their dreams for the school. Athens Clay Pullias and George Willard Collins were called upon to turn those dreams into reality.

Because of the controversy surrounding Ijams' departure, the board could not name the school's vice president, Pullias, as its president in 1943; too many fences had to be mended without and within. One of the great peacemakers in the history of the school and of the church, Batsell Baxter, returned to the presidency he had held for two years in the early thirties. Baxter knew he was an interim president, which pleased him: he was always happier preaching and teaching than in serving as a college president. He had previously been the chief administrator at Abilene Christian

College and at George Pepperdine College as well as at Lipscomb the two years before Willard Collins enrolled as a student.

Meanwhile the board—led by Chairman Harry Leathers and the powerful A. M. Burton—set its long-range plan into motion. Instead of sitting still or falling behind, Lipscomb was to grow into a four-year college with a strong faculty, solid finances, and a continued firm Bible base.

To set its ambitious program in motion, the board announced the formation of the Lipscomb Expansion Program in the fall of 1944. At its helm as director was Clay Pullias. The associate director was Willard Collins, a 29-year-old who had already established himself as a powerful preacher able to move people into action.

Collins was a familiar figure on campus when he accepted the work. He was serving as president of Lipscomb's Alumni Association, having replaced Judge Sam Davis Tatum in that role in June 1943. His wife Ruth, the first paid Alumni secretary, was writing Alumni Notes in *The Babbler.* Serving with Collins in alumni positions were Andy T. Richie, Jr., Mrs. Lacy Elrod, William Potts, Mary Emily Watkins, Norvel Young, Mrs. Lucy Sewell Fowlkes, Paul Moore, Clarence Dailey, and Mary Sherill.

As controversy deepened on campus, Collins was called in to help. He spoke at chapel on October 4, 1943, with the theme "We Must Depend on Some Power Greater than our Own." Eleven days later, when Ijams resigned after nine years in the presidency, the school called Collins to unite former students. He organized a successful alumni banquet and then joined men such as B. C. Goodpasture, John D. Cox, J. Marvin Powell, John Banister, H. Leo Boles, Ira Douthitt, Roy Cogdill, C. M. Pullias, T. Q. Martin, Marshall Keeble, and President Baxter in the "Sound Doctrine" theme of the lectureship.

As associate director of the "L.E.P." (Lipscomb Expansion Program), Collins continued to hold the title of president of the Alumni Association. He was on the road virtually every day talking with alumni and high school groups, asking for money for Lipscomb. He also recruited students to a school which was on its way to becoming a four-year college. Always there were speaking engagements at churches whose members were delighted to hear about the progress being made at the Nashville school.

The message Collins and Pullias carried was that David Lipscomb College had unlimited potential for growth and for teaching the Bible if it received the necessary financial support from those who believe in it.

The initial goal of the L.E.P. was to raise $600,000 to construct the facilities needed for a four-year college, especially an administration building with an auditorium, a gymnasium, and a library. Dormitory space was needed, too, since Elam Hall had been sub-divided to make room for the female students who dominated the enrollment during the war years. The physical plant at Lipscomb was the same one Willard Collins had known as a student a decade earlier. The six hundred thirteen students were crowded for living and studying space into Elam, Sewell, and Harding halls.

"Interested business leaders have offered $300,000 for the expansion program if the college can raise an equal amount," Pullias told the Nashville *Tennessean*. In actuality, "interested business leaders" translated primarily into Burton himself, the wealthy insurer whose vision and financial backing proved invaluable to David Lipscomb College throughout most of the twentieth century.

By February 2, 1945, over $86,000 had been raised. On March 24, Pullias and Collins announced that Chattanooga businessman B. A. Crisman and the estate of his brother, former board member Oscar A. Crisman, had pledged $70,000 for the building of Crisman Memorial Library.

On April 14, *The Babbler* said, "Pullias and Collins declared yesterday that they expect to visit every community, large and small, and give to each individual Christian an opportunity to contribute to the L.E.P."

"Both men were excellent speakers, and they were welcomed by congregations over a wide area," remembers Bob Kerce, the chairman of Lipscomb's mathematics department who was an aide travelling with the expansionists in the forties. "Collins used a simple presentation. He was persuasive and used more personal appeal than a logical approach. Pullias was more scholarly but not as entertaining. In those days, though, he could hold you on the edge of your seat with his speaking. They both were effective."

Most times, Kerce would bring the male quartet with him to perform at these functions, which were held at church buildings on a week night. Kerce recalls:

> The entertainment was good, with those speakers and singers in pre-television days. We would ask for money right then at every size congregation imaginable. People knew that's why they were there, and they were willing to give

to help build a church-related four-year college. Strong, powerful appeals were made; many times I wished I could give myself.

He added that a Lipscomb faculty member's salary precluded much of that.

By the end of March 1946, $458,939 had been collected and the goal raised to $750,000 within the next year. A long-range figure of one million dollars was being discussed. Under construction were the $311,000 administration building and auditorium, the $80,000 central heating plant and its accompanying tunnels, and the $190,000 Johnson Hall dormitory for women. On the drawing board were a $70,000 science building, a $100,000 physical education building and gymnasium, and $100,000 for site improvements, such as sidewalks.

Johnson Hall was the result of a $96,000 gift from Mrs. Helena Haralson Johnson, known as "Grandma Johnson" since Collins' first year on campus in 1934. An original investor in Burton's Life and Casualty Insurance Company, she had used her profits to benefit Lipscomb ever since she gave $1,000 in 1930 to help build Elam Hall. Later she gave $25,000 toward the erection of Sewell Hall, which became her home.

Meanwhile sportswriter Edgar Allen of the Nashville *Banner* wrote in his March 28, 1946, column of plans to build a $100,000 gymnasium on the David Lipscomb College campus. He said it would be "the city's finest." Funds were also raised to purchase fourteen acres for "Maplehurst Field" for future athletic expansion.

Throughout all of this growth and fundraising, Pullias and Collins emphasized the theme: "When the last brick is laid, the last dollar will be paid."

Collins shared an office with his fellow Marshall Countian, Margaret Leonard of the elementary faculty. He was listed as associate director of the Lipscomb Expansion Program, a teacher of social sciences, and a member of the Bible faculty that included John L. Rainey, S. P. Pittman, J. Ridley Stroop, C. L. Overturf, Ira North, Mack Craig, and its head, Athens Clay Pullias. In his first *Backlog* faculty appearance, he was appropriately pictured next to his recruiter and mentor, Miss Ora Crabtree.

The board of directors liked what was happening at David Lipscomb College; their faith in the two men they had selected to head the expansion program had been justified. In return, the board rewarded the hard-working duo by naming them to the school's top administrative positions.

In the spring of 1946, Batsell Baxter resigned the presidency to follow his "lifework of preaching." He became President Emeritus and assumed the Bible chair. On June 1, 1946, Clay Pullias was named president of David Lipscomb College; Willard Collins became vice president, only the second the school had ever known. It was an alliance that would remain intact for another thirty-one years.

The board immediately gave the Pullias-Collins team the nucleus of a faculty which would serve the school for decades. J. C. Moore, Jr., who had attended Lipscomb with Collins, accepted the position of business manager, while J. P. Sanders continued to serve as dean. Mack Wayne Craig came on the payroll four months after Collins. Two months later Dr. Batsell Barrett Baxter joined the faculty as chairman of the speech department after having taught six years at Pepperdine.

The board—which consisted of Leathers, Burton, M. N. Young, Sr., J. E. Acuff, S. H. Hall, I. C. Finley, James R. Byers, F. L. Williams, and James R. Tubb—added to the staff in 1947 J. E. Choate, Ralph Bryant, Margaret Carter, Bob Kerce, Ira North, Morris Landiss, Thomas Whitfield, and Sara Whitten, people who were to serve the school faithfully for decades. Already on the faculty were J. R. Stroop, Eugene "Fessor" Boyce, and Irma Lee Batey. A year later, Axel Swang and Ruth Gleaves came aboard.

Expansion efforts were productive not only in bringing in dollars but in recruiting students. The final two-year class graduated as President Baxter stepped down. In 1947-48 the first real senior class of the school—fifty-four in number—became a reality. In that group were future Lipscomb teachers Henry "Buddy" Arnold, John Holland, and Joe Sanders. Ruth Collins' brother, Bud Morris, was back for a bachelor's degree. In the junior class were men who were to become part of the faculty, including Edsel Holman, Nat Long, Leo Snow, and Paul Phillips.

David Lipscomb College was on the move. So was Vice President Willard Collins, one of the busiest men in Nashville.

A job description that was all-inclusive of Collins' duties during those three decades as vice president would be mindboggling. One press release called him "director of chapel services, publications, student recruiting, athletics, the Lipscomb Lectures, and the Artist Series. He assists the president in development; he is responsible for student life and behavior and is a member of the faculty of the Department of Bible."

If that was not enough, Willard Collins was on the road constantly as an evangelist. He could have properly been called "The Preaching Vice President." Pullias, Collins, and at least one other faculty member preached for years at a different congregation twenty-six of the fifty-two Sundays a year. That, of course, came after Collins gave up his located work with the Christians who met on Charlotte Avenue. Under an arrangement endorsed by Pullias with an itinerary of churches which the president approved, Willard Collins conducted thirteen gospel meetings a year, six of which had to be within driving distance of Nashville so that he could be on campus during the days, filling his other roles.

Soon the Lipscomb Press Bureau was issuing press releases saying, "Willard Collins probably comes as close to being known wherever churches of Christ have been established as any other man of our time." Cited as evidence for this claim were his countless appearances before audiences large and small throughout the United States and some foreign countries, his role as an administrator and Bible teacher at David Lipscomb College, his growing appearances over radio and television, and his widespread work as a writer.

Willard Collins the writer may have been overshadowed by Collins the speaker, but his byline on articles and his name on editorial staff lists were sought by most major Christian publications. He was on the editorial staffs of the *20th Century Christian*, the *Gospel Advocate*, and *Minister's Monthly*. He joined Ira North and Alan Bryan as the *Advocate*'s Centennial Committee, and he helped prepare advertisements for national magazines by serving on the editorial committee of the Gospel Press of Dallas, Texas. His weekly column in the Nashville *Banner* became a popular book, *Daily Living with Christ*. A number of his series of sermons were recorded in book form.

His voice became familiar even to those who did not attend his evangelistic meetings. He served as regular commentator for *Lipscomb Chapel Singing*, a program of recorded songs and Bible readings from daily chapel services aired regularly over thirty-three radio stations in twelve states. He appeared frequently on the Nashville television program *Know Your Bible* as a guest panelist along with regulars Charles Chumley, Sara Whitten, Charles R. Brewer, and moderator Ira North; he had joined Batsell Barrett Baxter in conceiving the idea for the program and then served as chairman of its program planning committee.

When the directors of the *Herald of Truth* asked Willard Collins to fill in for his friend, Dr. Baxter, on July 17, 1957, Dr. Pullias was so pleased that Lipscomb's vice president was chosen to speak over the three hundred-station network that he featured the news on the cover of *The Lipscomb Review*, a quarterly publication.

President Pullias, in fact, never missed an opportunity to praise the evangelistic work of his vice president. Having given up most of his preaching himself as the pressure of administrative duties continued to surround him, Pullias delighted in Collins' role as the preaching vice president. At least once a year the president wrote an article for the *Gospel Advocate* updating statistical data on Collins' evangelistic efforts, including baptisms, the large numbers of people hearing him from the pulpit, and his busy evangelistic schedule. By the summer of 1959, Pullias noted, Willard Collins had one hundred twenty-one meetings scheduled for the following decade. Very seldom did Collins conduct a meeting at a place that he was not asked to come back one or more times, the president was pleased to note.

With the support of the Charlotte Avenue congregation, which held both administrators in high esteem, Pullias directed the crowning achievement of the preaching vice president, the ultra-successful Collins-Craig Auditorium Meeting in Nashville.

The relationship between Clay Pullias and Willard Collins worked well for both men, especially through the sixties. Pullias was the unquestioned authority on campus, clearly the decision-maker for the school. Willard Collins was always in his shadow. "What you have to remember, though, is President Pullias pushed Brother Collins as the preacher, the voice of the administration in the pulpits of the country. That kept Brother Collins before the public and presented a good image of Lipscomb as well," says Carl McKelvey, Collins' choice as his original successor as vice president.

In a lengthy article praising Willard Collins, Pullias wrote in the June 25, 1959 *Gospel Advocate.*:

> Brother Collins' outstanding success as a gospel preacher witnesses that the word of God is still "quick and powerful." He proclaims God's word in all of its purity, and he preaches it from the heart. The combination of a powerful voice, a sincere appeal, and a personality that radiates love for his fellow man has made him one of the most powerful

preachers of our day.

What he has been able to do for the Lord in the pulpit during the past decade is little short of phenomenal. His achievements mark him as one of the great men of God in any time.

In that same article, President Pullias described his vice president's work as counselor and leader of young people, public relations director, director of Lipscomb Lectures, and a noted religious writer. He also could have talked about the Willard Collins the students knew from daily chapel.

If a poll of the thousands of alumni of David Lipscomb College were ever taken to determine what one phase of school life is most remembered, chapel might well be at the top. Undoubtedly that same poll would indicate that Willard Collins' role in chapel contributed to making it so memorable.

Every Lipscomb student not only takes a Bible class daily but also attends chapel services each school day. In addition to singing, prayer, and gospel messages, the time is used for announcements concerning school life and Christian living. During the school's approximately four decades as a senior college, the "master of ceremonies" and maker of announcements at chapel has been Willard Collins more often than not.

By appearing before the student body daily, Collins has helped unite those who were in the audience in their love of and their dedication to both the Lord and David Lipscomb College. He has used his personal magnetism and sincere Christian zeal to make those listening feel good about themselves, about their college, and about being a Christian.

Usually in the non-religious segment of his announcements, Collins has been able to get students and faculty alike to smile, often to laugh. Sometimes the laughter has been a result of a remark that elicited a double meaning for the listeners. These are often called his "Praise God and Buddy Arnold" statements and have become collectors' items.

"Now let us praise God and Buddy Arnold...will lead us in singing," Collins has often said, not realizing a misplaced pause has led the audience to grasp a different meaning from what Collins had intended. In fact, Arnold himself remains a part of those chapel memories.

"After brother Collins has said something that produces laughter,

you see him up on the platform whispering to Buddy Arnold trying to find out what's funny," says Steve Flatt, a vice president in
the Collins Administration who has become one of the top Willard
Collins impersonators of the eighties. "You can hear him asking
Buddy, 'What'd I say? What'd I say?'"

Among the most famous Collins lines are "Miss Gleaves and I
are going to stop parking on this campus" and "the faculty will
supply the ice cream, and Ruth and I will furnish the grass." In
the former, he was referring to his intention of joining Fanning Hall
supervisor Ruth Gleaves in reducing on-campus romancing, and
in the latter, he was making reference to a summer social being
held on the Collins yard. Listeners understood his meaning, too,
but that didn't stop mental pictures of a tryst between Collins and
the dorm matron or of the Collinses being suppliers of marijuana,
which had become known as "grass" in modern lingo.

Jim Mankin, the minister of the Madison Church of Christ, a Collins impersonator since his student days at Lipscomb, loves to repeat
a statement Collins made in chapel one morning after Lipscomb
students had spray-painted a building on another campus as a prank.
"Last night the worst thing happened at Lipscomb since I came,"
the vice president said.

"It is difficult to know which of the gaffes were real and which
intentional. He always manages to capitalize on them," says Dr.
Carroll Ellis, chairman of Lipscomb's speech department. Flatt notes
that Collins "feeds off" the laughter provided by his statements,
which would prove true by Collins' delight in having Flatt introduce
him with Willard Collins stories.

At the close of each chapel for decades, Willard Collins has
boomed in his marvelous voice, "That is all!" In the fall of 1985,
the ASA, which is so dear to his heart, sold "I Love Willard" buttons along with tee shirts with his face on the front and an in-
scription on the back reading: "42 Years of Service—That is All.'"

* * *

Lipscomb students also got to know the vice president as a teacher
of Bible. In addition to upper division courses for Bible majors, he
taught freshman Bible. Most of the new students at David Lipscomb
for decades had either Vice President Collins or Dean Mack Wayne
Craig as their first Bible teacher. The experience proved to be
uplifting.

"Class Note 101: It's a beautiful day!" Willard Collins was fond of telling his class as he emphasized the need for a positive attitude. That combination of words—"beautiful day"—was a phrase Lipscomb students longed to hear in the first two decades of Collins' tenure as vice president. Once a year, the administration would give the students an afternoon off for a schoolwide picnic at one of Nashville's parks. Buses would carry the students to Percy Warner, Edwin Warner, or Shelby parks where Fessor Boyce had planned activities at Collins' request. As students became more "sophisticated" and as the school grew, the idea Collins had carried over from his junior college love of May Day pleasures had to be abandoned in the mid-sixties. For those who were students in earlier years, Beautiful Day is one more fond memory of David Lipscomb College and of Willard Collins.

Every student's contact with Vice President Collins was not pleasant, though. As director of student life, the vice president also had the task of chairing the Student Welfare Committee. It became known as the "Farewell Committee," since the panel had the unpleasant task of student discipline, which could include suspension or expulsion.

The play on words concerning the committee appeared in the *Backlog* of 1946-47, which noted the "committee decides on the welfare or farewell of the students." In his first year as vice president, Collins' fellow committee members were dormitory supervisors Henry C. Ehl, Myrtle Parrish, and Maxine Feltman, along with Dean Sanders and Max Hamrick, principal of the high school.

Over the years, the composition of the committee has changed, but those who have served on it with Collins are virtually unanimous in their appraisal of his work.

"He has never been a villainous figure, even in discipline," Dr. Ellis says. "When he disciplined students, they left his office loving him. Carl [McKelvey] could take the same action when he succeeded Brother Collins, and the students would be furious at him. "'Why did you do it?' Brother Collins always asked the student, and they knew he really cared why."

"It was awfully hard for a student to sit and look at either brother Collins or Dr. Baxter and tell a lie," says faculty member Patty Dugger, a long-time committee member.

> Brother Collins had so much empathy for them, and it came across quickly, although he could never tolerate what they had done. He would explain the rules kindly. The

students never doubted he cared for them. When he asked "Why did you do it?" there was so much caring in his voice. The tone said, "bless your heart, why?" He brought tears to their eyes and to ours, too.

Fairness characterized the way Collins handled situations, Mrs. Dugger remembers. She says he always investigated cases when he learned of possible rule violations. She says he did not let the student's background get in the way of justice, adding:

> Even when he was emotionally involved, it never caused him to back off. He would say, "This is a sad case, but what can we do; folks, there's the rule." Many times he knew the parents, and he would say, "What is Joe [the father] going to say" or "What will that poor mother say?", but he never let anything slip by.

Fessor Boyce served on the committee and recalls:

> He hated sending someone home if he thought there was a chance to help them. A lot of students who gave trouble but were helped by that committee turned out to be fine men. Some of them are elders of the church today.

Finally in the late sixties, Vice President Collins received some relief from his job with the creation of the Dean of Students position. Thomas Cook was the first one to fill the role. He recalls the experience:

> He was still very much ready to help, but he never interfered. I made mistakes and would crawl to him for help. Somehow he would make me feel that what I had done was wonderful while he came up with a solution for the problem. He seemed to instinctively have the right answer. I was in the position four years and thought it was a horrible job. How in the world he maintained his sanity all those years amazes me.

Jim Thomas later served in the position and was amazed at Collins' "tremendous insight in dealing with the problems of students." Thomas continues:

His solutions are always so perfect and seem so obvious. He can drive through to the center of a problem and nail it down; he could solve a problem I had wrestled with for two or three weeks immediately, and his was the correct solution. He has a phenomenal talent for that. Yet I never received any "Jim, do it this way" instructions. He would lead me to a solution, but he wanted me to be convinced it was the best way to do it, not just his way.

While deans J. P. Sanders and Mack Craig developed the academic program, Willard Collins was building an athletic program that served as a model for other National Association of Intercollegiate Athletics (NAIA) schools.

As a student-oriented administrator, Collins devised a program for the entire student body. He called on the tireless Eugene Boyce to develop an intramural program that was second to none. Meanwhile, Coach Tom Hanvey was building a national powerhouse in gymnastics, a sport that involved few people but brought great acclaim to the school. Hanvey, a member of the NAIA's Hall of Fame, built a gymnastics team that was nationally known, twice finishing in the top four in the nation. Collins often had gymnasts perform for visiting groups as a recruiting tool. He frequently asked his hunting buddy, Hanvey, to take time out to visit churches to tell the young people of the wonders of David Lipscomb College. One of the saddest moments in the Collins presidency came when he agreed to drop gymnastics as a varsity sport after Tom Hanvey had retired and the sport had become a financial drain.

Other sports began to grow. Always a favored pastime on campus, even while Collins was a student, tennis became a winning tradition with some of Nashville's top professionals rising from Bison ranks. Coach Lynn Griffith had directed two teams to the national tournament in the eighties as Collins' final year in office began.

Coach Ralph Samples' golf teams became perennial district contenders and developed national prominence. Trophy cases in the student center are filled with track awards, and Coach Duane Slaughter brought honors to the school in badminton.

Collins oversaw the development of women's athletics on campus in an ever-widening circle. "I've noticed that brother Collins goes out of his way to attend women's basketball games whenever he can to show the girls he's behind them," says Mary Carrigan, secretary of the physical education department.

Those games are played in McQuiddy Gymnasium, one of the early products of the Lipscomb Expansion Program. Boyce says the 3,500-seat gym was "the best from Lexington (Kentucky) to the Gulf of Mexico" when first built. For a while, Vanderbilt University played its Southeastern Conference games in the facility, which brought recognition to the school.

Both Pullias and Collins attended basketball games faithfully. A good team was important to the school, since it was basketball that the alumni saw during homecoming. Fortunes of the team varied from year to year, but the Bisons were always competitive.

Two basketball highlights came in the mid-sixties under Coach Charlie "Tiger" Morris. The 1962-1963 Bisons not only became the first Nashville team to play an athletic event at that same Municipal Auditorium where Collins had been the featured speaker, but also won the game over outstanding opposition. Lipscomb beat Western Kentucky University 75-68 behind seniors John McCarley, Tracy Ramsey, George "Mac" Davis, Ron Sink, Ralph Isenberg, and Roland McDaniel. The Hilltoppers were coached by the legendary Ed Diddle, who failed to get win number 750 in this one against the much smaller school. Then Morris' 1966 team—led by Mike Hartness and Jackie Bradford—became the school's first twenty-game winner.

"It was in 1966 that brother Collins began saying 'On to Kansas City,' and he still says it a lot," remembers Ken Dugan, an assistant basketball coach at the time. Kansas City is the traditional site of NAIA national tournaments.

Dugan, Lipscomb's athletic director under Collins, is best known, though, for his success as a baseball coach. In the 1984-85 season Dugan won his eight hundreth ball game for his alma mater. A member of the NAIA Hall of Fame, Dugan's teams have won two national baseball championships and two national runner-up trophies among several national tournament appearances. In 1984 the baseball Bisons set an NAIA consecutive-wins record and tied an NCAA record with thirty-four straight wins.

"In 1971 and 1972, the two years we were national runner-up, brother Collins would call me every day in Phoenix, Arizona to discuss the games and how our players were doing," Dugan recalls. "He was vitally interested in not only our team but in the players. As president he has maintained that interest, even though he can't come to as many games."

Ken Dugan can laugh now about a traumatic experience in his

life involving Willard Collins.

In the late sixties I was coordinator of athletics and he was still chairman of the Athletic Committee. Guy Phipps of Union City had succeeded Tiger Morris as coach. One day, just before the season was to begin, I was studying at the Joint Universities Library at Vanderbilt working on my masters degree and got a call from brother Collins there. He said, "Phipps has quit! Phipps has quit! Get over here quick!" When I got to his office, President Pullias was on the phone, I believe from Cincinnati. Brother Collins told me to talk to him. I remember the president saying, "The first thing to do is calm Willard down." The next thing I had to do was be the basketball coach myself.

During those years, Dugan found athletes who could play basketball and baseball both, guys like Butch Stinson and Farrell Gean were to become the nucleus of the baseball dynasty.

Collins' concerns for basketball were made easier with the hiring of Don Meyer, one of the top coaches in the NAIA. Meyer built a basketball program that gained national recognition during the Collins Presidency, culminating in three trips to nationals in Kansas City in the first half of the eighties. Six Meyer teams during the first eight years Collins was president won twenty or more games. The 1985-86 Bisons won the NAIA national championship in March 1986.

All of this came from a school that had a 300-seat gymnasium when Willard Collins assumed the chairmanship of the Athletic Committee.

While not actively involved in athletics as a college student, young Willard Collins had been totally immersed in communications. In the written realm he served as president of the Press Club, business manager and columnist for *The Babbler*, and associate editor of the *Backlog*; he excelled in the spoken word as an orator, debater, and actor. Those experiences—along with his God-given ability as a preacher and his outgoing personality—helped him to be an outstanding public relations director for his school.

The 1958 *Backlog*, edited by future co-worker Dennis Loyd, and the 1959 yearbook, edited by Alvin Lewis Bolt, each called the vice president "the best public relations man that Lipscomb could have in most any respect." Close friend Franklin Camp calls him "the best public relations man I've ever known." Twice Collins was elected to the national board of the American College Public Relations Association.

Working primarily with Lipscomb News Bureau Chief Eunice Bradley through the years, Willard Collins sent out countless news releases about what was going on at David Lipscomb College, especially what its president, Athens Clay Pullias, was doing and saying.

Management of news was a time-consuming job at Lipscomb. Pullias was a great believer that Lipscomb publications should put forth a positive image to the alumni and public. He asked Willard Collins to help Miss Bradley see that that happened. "Brother Collins let me argue about what I thought," Miss Bradley remembers. "When it was over, he always won, but I had my say. Brother Collins generally thought whatever Brother Pullias thought about what should be in our papers."

Vice President Collins believed publications were the key to attracting many of the students to Lipscomb. In his final year as vice president, Collins was quoted in the *Backlog* edited by Becky Collins as saying:

> One of the most effective avenues of publicity is the printed page. Television is fine for immediacy; but the printed page continues to build images for years. People like to show me old *Backlogs* when I visit in their homes; therefore, I believe Lipscomb publications build Lipscomb on a permanent basis.

Collins-directed publications had played a role in attracting 2,154 students to enroll in the college in his final year as vice president, 1976-1977.

The Pullias Administration may have reached its height in the midsixties. A sixteen-page section appeared in The Nashville *Tennessean* Sunday, October 9, 1966, on the occasion of the celebration of the seventy-fifth anniversary of David Lipscomb College. "Lipscomb...Proud Past, Bright Future" the headline declared.

The expansion program had produced a $1.87 million science building, which was dedicated that day. Plans were announced for a dining complex/student center and a high rise dormitory. Forty-eight percent of the faculty had an earned doctorate with many more being encouraged financially to work toward that highest academic degree. Alumni and others were donating to the school in record numbers and amounts.

Willard Collins was a part of that success story. In fact, he had become Dr. Willard Collins, having been named a Doctor of Laws by Pepperdine College in 1968 because of "your efficient administration of your duties through twenty years as vice president, and your sincerity and humility—combined with your unselfish dedication to the advancement of the Kingdom among men."

Students had grown to appreciate him more and more. Editor Jane Gray dedicated the 1951 *Backlog* to Willard Collins noting:

> Love and appreciation for him grow with length of acquaintance. His life is sincerely devoted to the service of God. His love for the students is untiring, unselfish, and understanding. His tasks are without end and often without praise, but he does them faithfully for the benefit of the school and the glory of God. We believe that he exemplifies the true spirit of Lipscomb.

The 1959 *Backlog* said about Collins: "A big heart, ability to see the student's point of view, and an unwavering determination to do what is best in every case for the long range future of those concerned, have made him the personal friend of literally thousands of students and former students since he became vice president in 1946."

In the 1964 yearbook, this glowing appraisal of the vice president appeared:

> Eighteen years of service to thousands of students have endeared Willard Collins in the hearts of all who pass through the halls of this college. With a voice and appearance that command attention and respect, Lipscomb's Vice President has served as the untiring mediator between students and administration with a calm diplomacy that is rare. Faculty and students consider him a wise advisor...From under this awesome burden, Willard Collins emerges with a certain resiliency and sense of humor which reports confidently that the situation is well under control. Year after year he serves to make school policy run smoothly, transforming the somewhat chaotic influx of fourteen hundred undergraduates into a happy, healthy, cooperative working unit

All of those characteristics which had made Pullias and Collins successes were put to the test in the seventies. Three rocks upon which the expansion program had been built passed on. Board members I. C. Finley and A. M. Burton died within a ten-day period in the summer of 1966. Slightly over a year later, death claimed Board Chairman Harry Leathers. Finley had been on the board almost twenty-five years. Leathers was board chairman when Pullias and Collins were named directors of the LEP and then elected administrators. He had been highly supportive of Pullias.

No Tennessean had ever given more to any one institution than Andrew Mizell Burton did to David Lipscomb College. Estimates at the time of his death were that the insurer and his wife had donated over $3.5 million to the school, including $75,000 in his final year, the school's seventy-fifth.

It was Burton who had foreseen the need for a four-year college and who had provided the seed money to produce it. "He had the ideas and the money; it was the responsibility of Pullias and Collins to make his ideas become a reality," one associate says.

Although the Burtons left their valuable farm to Lipscomb, money did not pour into the school the way it had when A. M. Burton was alive. Churches and individual Christians were no longer giving in amounts needed to keep up with the demands of the school.

Pullias, who had a law degree and held an honorary doctorate, was respected in legal, financial, and political circles. He took active roles on many political issues and even considered becoming a candidate for public office. He never agreed to run for election, but he did become involved in leadership roles in issues facing Tennessee voters.

In the sixties, Pullias accepted a directorship of the Federal Home Loan Bank of Cincinnati. In 1968-69 he served as its chairman, an important and demanding position. It was a job which frequently took him away from Nashville.

In the seventies, Pullias maintained an office in his home and frequently worked there. That meant that Willard Collins was the administrator on campus whom people with complaints and problems came to see. "In many ways, he was acting as on-campus president without the title. In fact, he was Lipscomb's representative to meetings of college presidents for years before he had the title," notes Carl McKelvey.

In the mid-seventies, Willard Collins heard frequent complaints about the school from without and within. Although he tried to remain loyal to his friend and boss, Clay Pullias, Collins, too, was worried about the school they both had loved for decades.

For the first time since he had become a part of the staff in 1944, Willard Collins had doubts about the future of David Lipscomb College. He soon found out he was not alone.

Willard Collins as Vice President

Margaret Hopper, Mack Wayne Craig, Edsel Holman, Jackie Ray Davis,
Tom Hanvey, Athens Clay Pullias, and Willard Collins

Willard Collins and Governor Buford Ellington

''Classnote 101: It's a beautiful day!''

91

Chapter Six

The Christian Family

"Willard has become such a shameless name dropper! He begins every letter now 'Ruth and I...'" — Emma Staton.

The old cliche' "Behind every great man there is a great woman" not only holds true in the Willard Collins family but has been manifested four times over.

The large crowd gathered at David Lipscomb College for the Ruth Morris Collins Scholarship Dinner on November 21, 1985, paid tribute to the woman who has been "behind" Willard since that fateful bus trip to Cookeville fifty years earlier. Sitting by their mother's side were the two daughters who have shared the responsibility of trying to maintain family life with a father and husband who has been constantly on the road and who is among the most visible forces in the twentieth century.

If only Maxie Duncan Collins could have been alive to share the evening with her daughter-in-law, the women who have been so vital in Willard Collins' life could have made a foursome once again.

A quartet of sorts did entertain on this special night, when over $50,000 was raised for scholarships in Mrs. Collins' name. The four David Lipscomb College vice presidents sang a tribute to Lipscomb's first lady. Actually Carl McKelvey and Steve Flatt did most of the singing with Cliett Goodpasture and Earl Dennis offering quiet support. Flatt had written two songs in honor of Mrs. Collins. While both numbers drew good-natured laughter from those gathered, these words rang out as truths:

There's a lady named Ruth Collins
She's everything to him
She's the fairest of 10,000 to the school
She's the lily of the campus, the rose of Bison Square
In Willard's eyes she is the brightest jewel
As a mother she's a wonder
As a grandma she is swell
She is everybody's friend as a rule
She's the lily of the campus, the rose of Bison Square
In Willard's eyes she is the brightest jewel.

Although the spouses of many who have risen to the top go unnoticed, such has not been the case for Ruth Collins, especially in the years after her husband became a college president. The honor afforded her, though, has come from merit, not from her seeking or demanding it. Quiet and demure in public, Mrs. Collins has drawn an outpouring of praise, culminating on that special night in the November of her husband's final year in the presidency. The tributes resulted from widespread genuine appreciation for this Christian woman.

"When Brother Collins became president, Mrs. Collins told me that she was not to be referred to officially as 'the First Lady of Lipscomb' nor was her picture to appear in *The Babbler*," recalls Dr. Dennis Loyd, chairman of the English department in the final year of the Collins presidency, but faculty advisor for the student newspaper when the new president took office in 1977.

Frances Pullias had been quite visible during the four decades her husband had served the college as president. Her picture appeared regularly in *The Babbler* and a special room in the student center bore her name. Mrs. Collins made it clear that she did not want such publicity.

Instead she went to work behind the scenes, doing her part to help her husband set things aright for the school they both so dearly loved. Her approach—in addition to being a trusted but unofficial advisor to the president—was to serve as chief cook for special functions at the college.

"When Daddy accepted the presidency, he wanted to work with people on his level in a way he would be comfortable. Having Mother cook for them made him comfortable and her happy," says Corinne Collins Slayton. "The many thousands of dollars she has saved the school in doing the cooking is staggering. Jerry Clower [the country comedian who entertained at fund-raising banquets twice during the Collins years] was awed when he found out that the cook of a dinner he enjoyed so much was the president's wife."

Corinne's husband Ed told the crowd at the Ruth Morris Collins Scholarship Dinner that his mother-in-law is a wonderful cook. "Yet I learned long ago it is wiser not to ask her what is in a particular dish," laughed Slayton, referring to Mrs. Collins' penchant for experimentation in the kitchen.

On that evening when Ruth Collins was the featured attraction and Willard merely her guest, the former alumni secretary and *Babbler* editor was praised by those on the program. Included among those who gave tributes were Jim Bill McInteer, Henry Arnold, Joe Sanders, All Student Association president Tim Gobble, her brother Bud, and women from the sponsoring Associated Ladies of Lipscomb. Those who spoke were President Marjorie Scobey, ALL founder Gerry Ezell, Ruth Byers, Annette Johnson, Shirley Bramlett, Nell Wilkerson, and chairwomen Dianne Olive and Emma Staton. Alice Ann Chapman, a family friend, represented her boss, Mayor Richard Fulton, in declaring November 21, 1985, "Ruth Collins Day" in Metro Nashville.

Yet no special evening or fund-raising event is needed for people to sing the praises of the transplanted Georgian. A sampling follows:

Joe Sanders (long-time family friend and retired faculty member)—'If it weren't for Ruth, there wouldn't be a Willard;"

Bob Neil (faculty member during Willard and Ruth's days as Lipscomb students)—'Willard has been fortunate to have the backing of a very able wife; he has had no domestic worries to keep him from concentrating on preaching and on Lipscomb;"

Board member Lee Marsh—'She is the finest lady a college president could have for a wife; we got two for the price of one;"

Jim Bill McInteer (minister and 20th Century Christian president and publisher)—'Ruth has been a tower for Willard and for Lipscomb;"

Robert Kerce (a Morris family friend from Atlanta and DLC mathematics department chairman)—'Ruth is so intelligent; she has given complete support to her husband's talents;"

Faculty member Buddy Arnold—'She has a marvelous, unaffected nature with no pretense and a genuinely gracious, loving spirit;"

Metro Councilman Tandy Wilson—'Mrs. Collins makes people feel relaxed. She and her husband are among the few people who can make you want to help them without their asking. A husband and wife team that can get things done."

* * *

Willard Collins is well aware of how special his wife is and of what she has done for him and for Lipscomb. Yet he says, "Even though I've enjoyed the food and all that, Ruth's greatest accomplishment is rearing the family."

Indeed, during his daughters' formative years, Willard Collins worked day and night for the Lord and for Lipscomb. He shared "quality time" with Carole and Corinne, but most of the household responsibilities and the day-to-day decisions that must be made in every family fell on Ruth.

Carole, the older daughter, still feels that she missed out on some childhood joys by her father's being gone so much. Corinne, on the other hand, cherishes the times she shared with her dad when he was at home. The girls—now women in their forties—readily agree that these opposing perceptions are characteristic of their differences.

"Carole is so much like me that it's hard to live with her," President Collins confided to the crowd at the Ruth Collins dinner. "We thought for a time Corinne wouldn't make it; we thought Carole would kill her."

Corinne says, "I see my Mother and Daddy as one—a matched set. Yet Carole has all of Daddy's goal setting and keep-going tendencies while I have Mother's hominess. You can tell a little about us by where we settled. Carole lives in the big city (Atlanta). I stayed close to the family in a small town (Franklin, Tennessee)."

Carole Collins Demonbreun has a masters degree in exceptional children from Penn State University and a Specialist in Education degree from Middle Tennessee State University in administration and supervision. She has taught in both public and private schools, including serving as principal of Middle Tennessee Christian School for two years. At the time of her father's retirement, she was serving as director of the Exceptional Student Program at Greater Atlanta Christian School, working with both the gifted and the slow learner.

Corinne Collins Slayton graduated from David Lipscomb College, as did her sister. Corinne's degree is in home economics, and she has been most content in using that degree as a homemaker, wife, and mother.

The sisters have much in common. They both married Lipscomb

men before their graduations. Both of their husbands are educators and both have been ministers. Each has two children, all four of whom are bright, good-looking achievers. And all four members of each family are close and devoted to Willard and Ruth Collins. Yet they have opposing evaluations of their childhoods as the children of Willard Collins.

"When I was real little, we lived in Old Hickory before Daddy went to work for Lipscomb. He was around more then. I can remember his going to an old railroad bridge with me; we'd throw rocks and play," says Carole, who was born during the local evangelism days on December 11, 1941, the week of the bombing of Pearl Harbor that precipitated America's entry into World War II.

"By the time we started school, he was working at Lipscomb and was gone most of the time. I remember that when he was going to be home at night, we couldn't have people over. Our family was built around his time."

Carole was always aware of the responsibility she carried as a student at David Lipscomb. "If a teacher ever said to Carole, 'What would your Daddy think?' or 'I know you'll do this for us because you're Willard Collins' daughter,' then that teacher was no longer one of Carole's favorites, to say the least," Ruth Collins remembers.

"I think I had 'P. K. S.,' Preacher's Kid Syndrome," Carole remembers with a laugh. "I felt that I couldn't be a typical teenager as Willard Collins' daughter."

Bob Demonbreun says his wife was reluctant for him to continue preaching while their children, Bryan and Tasha, were growing up because of her experiences as a preacher's child.

"I think it was fortunate that we both were girls, since we were with Mother so much while Daddy was on the road. Lipscomb sent him where no one else wanted to go and Mother stayed home with us. I realize now that as soon as we were grown, she started going everywhere with him. She had stayed home for us."

Corinne, born November 1, 1943, remembers things differently.

> I never recall feeling cheated when Daddy wasn't home. I just remember how much I enjoyed the time he was with us. Daddy would watch television with me. I remember our watching Red Skelton and Groucho's *You Bet Your Life* together. I loved for him to come home for lunch, since he was so much fun.
>
> When he was at home, it was quality time. I really did

like being his daughter; I adore him. But I never had any doubt about what came first in his life. In his mind, the church and the school are almost synonymous.

Corinne recalls another contrast in the way the girls handled their status: "Carole did her best to keep people from knowing her relationship with Daddy, but I'd go by his office and leave my books there."

Both daughters were popular students. Corinne was elected secretary of the student body in 1963-64; Carole had been runner-up in the voting for Miss Lipscomb the year before.

Like her dad almost two decades earlier, Corinne had given her folks cause for concern whether she would ever be a student. "I have this vivid recollection of them having to peel me off Daddy's leg when he took me to school the first day," she says.

Carole recalls the scene, too: "I can remember standing at the pencil trimmer in the third grade when Miss Leonard [now Mrs. Margaret Hopper] came after me to quiet Corinne down. It wasn't something I wanted to do." "Well, she wasn't the one I wanted either," Corinne counters with a laugh.

The girls were close, though; the entire family was. Summers signaled long trips to distant states where Willard Collins could not preach his sermons during the school year. Often, one or more friends were invited to go along. "Over the years, we traveled from Maine to Washington state. I learned to drive a car going across the desert in the West. By the time Corinne and I married, we had been in forty-three states," Carole recalls.

Frequent trips to Florida were on the agenda. The Sunshine State has always held an attraction to Willard Collins, and its people— who gave him his first regular preaching position in the summer of 1935—have invited him back time after time.

"I can remember thinking there must not be any members of the Church of Christ in Florida, since we went mixed swimming in the ocean. We weren't allowed to do that in Nashville," Corinne says with the same mischievous grin that little Willard must have used in plotting childhood capers with Frank Medearis.

That family resemblance was of great comfort to little Corinne when it dawned on her how much she looked like her grandmother, Maxie Collins. "Up until then, Carole just about had me convinced that I was adopted," she chuckles.

The girls got to know their Collins grandparents well. The

Nashvillians tried to visit Collins Hollow twice a month. Sometimes Carole and Corinne spent nights with Walter and Maxie Collins while their parents were gone. Both cherish the memory of Willard Collins seeing to it that his parents had indoor plumbing. Not only was it good for the grandparents but it also made their visits more comfortable. Corinne once held a television in her lap from Nashville to Lewisburg on one of her dad's missions to modernize his parents' home.

During the school year, family visits to Atlanta to see the Morrises usually came on holidays, especially Christmas. During the summers the girls took turns spending lengthy periods with "Pop and Nanny."

As his granddaughters reached college age Frank Morris suffered a crippling stroke that took much of his wife's time. Corinne recalls driving her grandfather around Atlanta for hours at a time to give her Nanny some freedom. It was during these prolonged stays in Atlanta that Carole decided the hometown her mother had abandoned in 1933 would be a wonderful place to live.

There were times, however, that Carole disdained separation from her parents. Paul Morrison, a leader in the church at Old Hickory, recalls that for the first three years of her life, Carole cried most of her waking moments. "I remember knocking on their door one time and Ruth rushing to ask me to please be quiet; she had just gotten Carole to sleep," Morrison recalls. Later Carole went through what her psychology-trained husband calls "separation anxiety." She begged her mother not to leave her or to travel with her father for fear of an automobile accident. Finally a pediatrician convinced her to "trust in God to take care of your parents."

Later she had advanced to the stage where she could spend a week at the home of Chester Jaynes near the Charlotte Avenue church. She rode a bus to Lipscomb to school that week and credits the experience for helping her break her fear of separation.

Then came a point in Carole's life when she thought she wanted to go away from home to college, as her parents had done before her. "I was considering going to Ole Miss with my friend Mary Farrar Cayce. Then I met Bobby and everything changed," she says.

Bob Demonbreun, an outstanding student and leader, and Carole Collins began dating in 1959 in high school. They both decided to attend David Lipscomb College and knew that marriage was in their future. "I probably would have lived in the dormitory, but Bob and I were saving all the money we could for marriage," she says.

99

What should have been one of the happiest times of Bobby's and Carole's years at Lipscomb turned into a family problem that a lesser father than Willard Collins would have had trouble handling. Demonbreun was elected president of the student body his senior year. At a dinner in the student center early in the year, Bob made traditional remarks. Among them was a pledge to the effect that the students would band together and be united to improve student morale.

President Pullias was incensed by the remarks and accused the young man of attempting to lead a rebellion. Many at that dinner still recall the evening with a shudder. The veteran administrator strongly expressed his anger that night. After a meeting between the college president and the student body president the following day, Demonbreun says that Pullias never spoke to him nor shook his hand again.

"Brother Collins never bad-mouthed President Pullias. He apologized to me for what had happened and he tried to smooth things over. I know it hurt Carole's mom and dad very much," Demonbreun says almost a quarter of a century later.

Bob Demonbreun never felt as close to Lipscomb as he once did after that. Yet when Willard Collins ascended to the presidency in 1977, he talked with his older son-in-law repeatedly about the challenges facing him and the college. Demonbreun, who holds a Ph.D. in clinical psychology from Penn State, is director of special services for a prominent Atlanta health group.

Ed Slayton came to Lipscomb from Atlanta, but is a country boy at heart. He says it never intimidated him that he was dating the vice president's daughter. "I do remember all of the jokes about how well lighted the Lipscomb campus was. Their home was the same way. I always thought I was at the Lealand Lane Airport when I took Corinne home," he laughs.

That house on Lealand Lane became the Collins home in 1954, when Willard and Ruth bought the 2.7-acre site for $23,000. They soon discovered that the reasonable price might have been aided by an official of the Ku Klux Klan living nearby. "He was very nice to us after he found out that Willard was a preacher," Mrs. Collins recalls. The girls would invite their school friends over to watch the Klan gatherings and parades in the neighborhood.

The first official residence of Mr. and Mrs. Willard Collins was in the Jacksonian Apartments at Old Hickory. The couple moved there in August 1939, after an extended honeymoon that included

100

staying with Henry and Gerty Haislip during a meeting at Catalpa in rural Tennessee. They traveled to Prairie Hill, Oklahoma, where Willard preached a meeting. They stayed with Bonnie and Earl Smith while there.

The marriage could have been short-lived. While they were in Oklahoma, Smith, the minister of the congregation, lost control of his vehicle and collided with a beer truck. The newlyweds were his passengers. "We just bounced back into the ditch and weren't hurt," Mrs. Collins remembers.

The first home the Collinses owned was also in Old Hickory. Most houses in "The Village" were owned by Du Pont, the company which employed members of many of the families in the congregation. Willard and Ruth, however, found a little white house on Concrete Road nearby. With a loan of $3,000 from well-known minister Ira Douthitt, they became homeowners.

It was in his new role as head of the household that Willard Collins convinced all who came into his presence that he had lost all of the manual dexterity he had possessed as a Marshall County farm boy.

"I remember that when Lee Gross and I helped him move in I found that he had no mechanical ability," Joe Sanders laughs. "If you send him to get a screwdriver, he may bring back a claw hammer. He couldn't screw a light bulb in. He thought I could do anything after I stopped his basement from flooding. Long after he encouraged me to go to college and to become an educator, he told people, 'I'm the only man in Nashville with a Ph.D. for an electrician.'"

Collins also has joked about having a Ph.D. as a groundskeeper after the move to Lealand Lane. "He hired our sons, Tom and Jeff, to mow his yard, since we lived nearby," remembers Dr. Thomas Whitfield, long-time chairman of Lipscomb's education and teacher training departments. "Sometimes when the boys weren't able to be there, I would mow it for them. Then Willard would joke about my being hired to take care of his yard."

The people of Old Hickory—regardless of their educational level—took the young couple under their wings. Especially concerned were Mr. and Mrs. F. W. Jaynes, who ran a grocery near the Jacksonian Apartments. Mr. Jaynes was an elder at Old Hickory and his wife was a Kentucky farm girl who knew how to rear a big family. Two of their sons, Allen and Chester, were to become elders of churches at Ashwood and Charlotte Avenue. Old Hickory was indeed a "Family of God."

Some of the nurses at Madison Hospital once tried to give Joe Sanders credit for being even more a part of the family than he was. Carole Ruth Collins (the first name came from the holiday season) had been born at Madison, December 11, 1941 with Daddy nearby. However, on November 1, 1943, as Corinne neared her arrival, Willard Collins was urgently summoned to speak at chapel services at David Lipscomb College where things were in turmoil over the premillennialism issue. Collins first checked his wife into the hospital and then heeded Norvel Young's appeal to get to the school quickly.

After making the speech, Collins called the hospital and learned of the birth of Anne Corinne. The young preacher already had reservations on the Pan American train that would take him to speak in a 10-day meeting for the Strathmoor congregation in Detroit, Michigan. "Tickets were hard to get in the war years. I also felt an obligation to do my part, since so many families were separated during the war. When I found out that Ruth and the baby were all right, I took the train to Detroit and didn't see Corinne until she was almost two weeks old," he remembers.

The folks at Old Hickory, meanwhile, continued to care for the young mother. Joe Sanders frequently visited the hospital. Observing the baby's fair locks and Sanders' blonde hair, one nurse said, "She looks just like her father," not realizing Willard had never seen his baby.

The Collinses have told the story frequently, and Sanders himself mentioned it at the Ruth Morris Collins Scholarship Dinner. It was a tribute to both families that the story could be told without it being tainted with any suggestion of being "dirty."

When Collins accepted work with Lipscomb, the family moved from Old Hickory to Nashville. (In pre-metropolitan government days, residents of Davidson County did not consider themselves as living in Nashville unless they were closer to downtown.) The Collinses purchased a house at 907 Woodmont Boulevard, only about three blocks from the Lipscomb campus. Then came a move six years later in 1951 to the other side of DLC on Temple Avenue. There they stayed until the purchase of the Lealand Lane home in 1954.

After Collins resigned from his work at Charlotte Avenue and from located preaching, the Collinses placed their membership at the Granny White Church of Christ, which had been the College church when they were Lipscomb students. "There were a lot of young people at Granny White then for Carole and Corinne to be with, and the girls and I needed a church home close to us while Willard was on the road," Mrs. Collins explains. The Collinses have attended Granny White ever since.

A few women have played a role in Willard Collins' life besides his mother, his wife, his daughters, and teacher Ora Crabtree. Most notable are his secretaries, women such as Betty Knott, Mabel Harding Bean, Mary Ella Ryan, Jamie Ussery, and Dianne Olive.

Also contributing to the family's well-being has been Dona Majors, a black lady from near Mt. Juliet, Tennessee, who started helping Ruth around the house shortly before Carole was born. When the Collinses moved to Nashville, she continued to help, most often spending three days and two nights with the young family before returning to her Wilson County home. A year older than her employers, who have been like family to her, beloved Dona was still working one day a week for the Collinses in the final year of the Collins presidency.

Willard and Ruth were also able to be around her mother more in their later years. Mrs. Morris moved to Nashville in the late sixties, making her home with her son Bud and his wife Betty. In recent years, "Nanny" has been confined to nursing homes but gets frequent visits from her family.

In addition to his daughters, Willard Collins has been administrator while other Morris descendants have been students. Bud and Betty Morris' two sons, Bob and Dick, are Lipscomb graduates, and Bob is now the Collins' dentist. A sister, Lynn, graduated from the high school. Ruth's sister, Martha Kate "Chick" Hammond and her late husband, J. B., sent four children to Lipscomb, basketball player Mike, David, Becky, and Jenny.

Although Collins has performed wedding ceremonies for countless couples throughout his career, he did not do the honors for his daughters. He gave Carole away in an August 1963 West End ceremony at which Carroll Ellis, Batsell Barrett Baxter, and Mack Wayne Craig presided. He did play a bigger role in the August 20, 1965 wedding of Corinne and Ed, but Carl McKelvey performed the actual ceremony.

Corinne and her mother were featured in a color photo section of *The Tennessean* four days before her wedding by Foods Editor Bernie Arnold, a Lipscomb graduate. Mrs. Arnold wrote what visitors to Lipscomb during the Collins presidency were to learn on their own: "Ruth Collins is a wonderful cook."

Among all the young people who have loved and admired Willard Collins during his forty years at Lipscomb, none could compare with the four teenagers descended from him. The grandchildren of Willard and Ruth Collins are intensely devoted to their "Granddaddy" and "MaRu." (MaRu came from Bryan Demonbreun, the eldest, shortening "Mama Ruth.")

As President Collins prepared to pass his position to Harold Hazelip, only one of the four, 16-year-old Mark Slayton, was a student at David Lipscomb, where he was a high school junior. Bryan and Tasha Demonbreun, students at Greater Atlanta Christian School, say they wish they could attend the school while their grandfather was president.

"When Bryan came home from high school day at Lipscomb in his junior year, he talked about how much everyone loves his Granddaddy," Carole says. "He was disappointed that he wouldn't get to be there with him, but I assured him that as long as Granddaddy lives he will be around that campus." The first of the grandchildren, Bryan, born in 1967, would enter David Lipscomb College in the fall of 1986.

Mark says most of his peers at the high school are not aware of who his grandfather is. "I don't make it a point to tell them; it's not a big issue. I'm not ashamed of it, though. In fact, I'm proud of him. I was really proud the day President (Gerald) Ford came to campus (for an assembly of all the student bodies in addition to invited guests November 4, 1985) and everybody saw him there with my Granddaddy," says Mark, who drops by Collins' office occasionally as his mother did before him.

Mark's brother Mike, the youngest of the grandchildren, born in 1971, was completing Northside Junior High School in Brentwood while his granddad was in his final year in the presidency. Ed Slayton is assistant principal of the school in addition to serving as minister of the Millview Church of Christ near Franklin. In a major paper for her degree in home economics, Corinne Collins had written that the ideal time for a youngster to begin Christian education was at the high school level, and she has continued that belief as a mother. Mark had gone to public schools in Williamson County before entering Lipscomb High.

Meanwhile Tasha Demonbreun, a year older than her cousin Mike, was the most removed from being on campus with her grandfather. A talented athlete, she was a freshman at Greater Atlanta

Christian in 1985-86. Tasha, like the others, however, has spent many happy moments with her grandparents.

"He's always taken us to movies. Usually he falls asleep and then tries to pretend he watched them, or he'll go get the food," she says. "If it's a comedy, he can stay awake. Then he'll likely go to sleep driving us home."

The grandchildren remember going on walks with their grandparents. Actually the Collinses walked and the youngsters rode the Big Wheels and "green machines" kept at Lealand Lane for their use. The Slayton and Demonbreun children talked about the paths as "Spooky Street, Curvy Street, Hilly Street, and Noisy Street."

Inside the Collins home were adventures with games, cartoons, and Rook. The dignified college president was open game for his grandchildren, who lovingly called him "Willardene" or "Uncle Willard." A favorite pastime involved putting up Granddaddy's hair in curlers.

The older two, Bryan and Mark, got to go along with their grandparents on a 10-day tour of Alaska during the summer of 1984. They had their own room on a cruise ship. "You'd think it would be boring being with all of their friends who are older, but we had an absolute blast with them," Bryan says. "Granddaddy and MaRu" have invited Tasha and Mark to join them on a European trip as they grow older.

Mark and Mike have the advantage of living closer to their grandparents. Mike and Granddaddy often go out alone for stops at D'Lites and Bojangle's restaurants. Krystal once was a favorite stopping place, but the putt putt miniature golf course adjacent is no longer there. Bryan and Tasha come to Nashville whenever possible. They got to be with their grandparents the week before Thanksgiving (because of the MaRu's special night) and during Thanksgiving in 1985. The Collinses went to Bob's family's home at Columbia, Tennessee., on Christmas Day for a joint family gathering.

Whenever the children spend the night with their grandparents Collins, they can hear the comforting sound of Willard Collins' snoring. "He snores like a freight train," Bryan says. Mike adds, "You wake up thinking a tornado has come through. He says it's MaRu, but we know better."

The sounds coming from "Uncle Willard" during the wee hours of the morning are not always of the snoring variety. He has a reputation for being a great midnight snacker, or, any other time, for that matter. Mrs. Margaret Clayton remembers that as a young minister preaching in Chattanooga young Willard asked for a bowl of hard-boiled eggs. Then as he studied his sermon, he peeled and ate the eggs.

Collins is best known for his penchant for grapes and Goo Goo chocolate cluster candy from Nashville-based Standard Candy Company, although not necessarily at the same time. "Mom can't win on Goo Goos," Ed Slayton told the crowd gathered to honor his mother-in-law on Ruth Collins Night. "If she doesn't have them, Dad says, 'There's nothing in the house to eat.' If she does keep them, he says, 'Law me, Ruth, how do you expect me not to gain weight?'"

Weight, strangely enough, has not been much of a problem for the stocky man from Marshall County, despite his being treated to countless home-cooked meals by great hostesses across the nation. He weighed 170 pounds at marriage and hasn't varied too much from that since.

Perhaps one reason he has been able to maintain his "figure" is that he has no idea how to prepare his own meals. Willard Collins is as helpless in the kitchen as he is in the workshop. "Where do we keep the glasses, Ruth?" he has asked often in the house the Collinses have called home for over thirty years.

The "Spilled Peas Incident" is perhaps as great a piece of Willard Collins folklore as are his chapel goofs. The story has been repeatedly told as the gospel about the college administrator trying to get something out of the refrigerator, overturning a bowl of peas, and then leaving the evidence on the kitchen floor to be disposed of by his wife.

In general it would appear that his appetite has not affected Collins' health. For most of his life he has experienced little sickness, probably based in part on his fear of having to go to the doctor if he should become ill. He inherited from his dad Dump Collins his distaste for visiting doctors' offices.

That had to change, however, when he began experiencing problems with his vision in 1967. The Collinses became concerned when family friend Mrs. Howard (Maxine Feltman) White suffered eye cancer. He went to see his friend and optometrist Dr. Lee Cayce in 1968 and immediately received a chiding for not having been there for eight years. Glaucoma was the diagnosis.

Treating Collins' vision then became a family concern. Drops were tried and then a medicine which Collins says "changed my personality." His wife says quietly, "He was a little fussy." Students at Lipscomb tried to help out by driving him to his evening speaking engagements. By the fall of 1972, Collins could no longer see overhead signs. He knew something had to be done.

Surgery removed the cataracts at Baptist Hospital in January of 1973. The operation was a success. It was the early eighties before Collins had any more trouble with his eyes.

Ruth Collins became seriously—perhaps deathly—ill in 1980. She underwent gall bladder surgery that led to complications. Two weeks later, family physician Dr. Ralph Massey diagnosed her problem as pancreatitis and alerted the hospital emergency room to be ready to treat it. "We've been told that Dr. Massey's quick and proper diagnosis saved my life," Mrs. Collins says gratefully.

Massey and chiropractor Dr. Lawrence Adams have done most of the medical work for Ruth Collins over the years. Nevertheless, she and her husband both decided it was time to get on a preventive medical program after her close call. Illnesses suffered by friends Batsell Barrett Baxter and Ira North made the Collinses more aware of the need to stay healthy.

Mrs. Ed Smith, the former Mary Ann Thomas of Lewisburg, became interested in Ruth Collins' health after Mrs. Collins contracted pancreatitis, the disease which had claimed the life of her husband, a Lipscomb board member. She told the Collinses of Dr. Marshall Ringsdorff of the University of Alabama School of Dentistry, who has done extensive research in health maintenance. And it was Baxter himself who got the doctor's address for the Collinses.

Willard and Ruth now faithfully follow the regimen prescribed by the Alabama doctor. It involves closely monitoring the body's intake of water, air, and food along with exercise. A machine takes the impurities out of the air they breathe in their bedroom. The Collinses walk at a rate of 120 paces per minute, and they chew their food 15 to 20 times a bite. They restrict their intake of caffeine, white flour, white sugar, and saturated fats. Their water comes from Minnesota; their vitamins are imported from California, their meat from Omaha, Nebraska. When Willard Collins sits down to a meal in the Lipscomb Dining Center, waitresses automatically place buttermilk at his plate. "I guess that is one advantage I take of my position," laughs the man who has steadfastly refused to have his own reserved parking place. While this may seem "silly" to some, Willard Collins says simply, "It works; it makes us feel good."

All of this, of course, is more expensive than the average diet or style of living. Over the years, the Collinses have allowed themselves few luxuries, though. "I think they have enjoyed some of the things they could not afford in the past," Corinne says of her parents. "But I remember when Mother went to Watkins Institute to learn how to sew our clothes for us better. She has always had to write the checks and balance the checkbook. She deserves to have some good things now." Ed Slayton agrees that his father-in-law enjoys what he calls "going first class."

Throughout his life, the farm boy from Marshall County has been impressed by success, whether it was the political style of Lewisburg lawyer/governor Jim McCord or the evangelistic style of a Foy E. Wallace, Jr., or a Marshall Keeble. He is especially in awe of successful businessmen. Steve Flatt loves to entertain with tales of "Willardese" about Collins' reaction to others' worldly possessions.

Willard Collins would be the first to say that he's the richest man alive, though. He has had a lifelong love affair with the Lord, His church, and the school which tries to teach young people to share that love and to be successful Christians in today's world.

And Willard Collins has long been rich in having a loving wife, lovely daughters who love him, and four adoring grandchildren. He is rich indeed as the patriarch of a Christian family.

Words which Athens Clay Pullias wrote about the Collinses in 1961 ring true today. "I know of no family anywhere that is setting a nobler example of what the Christian home was intended to be."

Willard and Ruth Collins

Carole, Corinne, Ruth and Willard

Chapter Seven

An Interview with Willard Collins

It is difficult for a writer to capture all the important ideas and concepts of a person in a narrative. Sometimes it is best to allow that person to speak for himself. This chapter is an edited version of a lengthy interview with Willard Collins. It allows Collins to speak for himself on several topics that are of special importance to him.

—Robert E. Hooper

Hooper: President Collins, you are goal-oriented. How important are goals to success?

Collins: I feel that enthusiasm and goal-setting go hand in hand. I've never seen much accomplished without enthusiasm. When a congregation is dead, it's dead. It's next to impossible for a dead congregation to grow. You must have enthusiasm and goal-setting helps build enthusiasm. The people want to reach that goal and then they become enthusiastic. And so at Old Hickory we set Sunday school goals. At Madison, Ira North set Sunday school goals and he built the church. Without enthusiasm you don't accomplish much.

Hooper: You were very successful at Old Hickory in encouraging young men to preach. Why did five or more young men choose to preach in your five years at Old Hickory?

Collins: I guess some of the most productive work I ever did was in local work at Old Hickory. If I had to go back in my life and pick out the most productive period in my church work, it'd be Old Hickory in getting boys to preach. First, we started them out early. We'd get them up on their feet. Soon they'd be reading and speaking. Second, the parents were so happy when their boys thought about being preachers. It was just thrilling for those parents at Old Hickory for a boy to want to preach.

They loved Brother Harper, they loved Brother Garner. They appreciated what I was doing in the church there, and preaching was just tops for them in regard to their sons. The parents were glad for daughters to marry preachers.

Today it's different. Parents want boys to go into business and want their daughters to marry businessmen or lawyers or doctors. There's a different attitude entirely. Churches must start early with classes. Keep those boys active in the church.

Hooper: Old Hickory and Charlotte Avenue were both vibrant churches in the 1930s and the 1940s and on into the 1950s. What part did local leadership play in this success?

Collins: A congregation is no more effective than its eldership. I really feel that if you've got an eldership that turns down plans, you've got an eldership that doesn't want to grow. It's an eldership that's afraid to do anything. It's difficult for a preacher to do anything.

Hooper: What do you perceive as the relationship between the school and the church?

Collins: The church, as I understand it from the New Testament, has the universal side and the local side. When the Lord adds people to the church, he adds to the church universal. Then you in your own preference decide which congregation you'll become a member of. I think I'm a member of the church when I'm working at Lipscomb. I've always thought that. I am working at Lipscomb as a member of the church. I am a member of the Granny White congregation, but I'm working at Lipscomb as a member of the church.

But the school is different from the church. It's not a congregation, but the school is a training ground for Bible school teachers, husbands and wives, preachers, elders and deacons. It's one of the best training grounds I know. It's a good training ground for mission work. A Christian school teaches the Bible. I think of the school as a group of members of the church from different congregations working together to train people for a life in the church and for eternity.

Hooper: The school, therefore, is a benefit to the church.

Collins: Yes. You train the teachers, you train the elders, you train the preachers, you train the mission people in a school like Lipscomb. I could preach for a local church, but here I can train fifty boys a year. When I first came to Lipscomb I had a Monday night class for preachers. I never will forget that. I taught them how to baptize. I taught them the methods of local work.

Hooper: The post-World War II era was a great period of religious activity. In looking back at that era, how would you describe it in relationship to churches of Christ?

Collins: The religious fervor was much stronger, and the churches of Christ were right in the middle of it. This was one of the fastest growing periods I've seen in the churches of Christ.

The church caught the enthusiasm. Military men came back from the war and wanted to do mission work. They wanted to help convert Europe and wanted to help convert this country. The mission fever spread over the local church. They came back with a renewed zeal that this world needed Christ and needed peace.

People came to meetings. They were glad to come to church together. They rejoiced in it. Some of the biggest meetings I ever had were right after World War II closed. I baptized 111 in twelve days at Old Hickory. The buildings were full. Children sat all around the pulpit stand. We'd have chairs in the aisles. And on a few occasions people would stand around the wall to hear preaching. They really believed that Christ was the way to peace. They'd been through such a turmoil and so much danger.

I used to catch a plane at 2:30 in the morning out of Fort Worth, returning home to Ruth and the children after closing meetings on Sunday night somewhere in Oklahoma or Texas. I remember this black man wiping and sweeping the floor of that airport while I was waiting on that 2:30 a.m. plane. I said, "What does it take to bring people together? What, do you think, does it take to bring races together? What does it take to bring people together in a country like this?" He said, "Tragedy." He said it takes some kind of great tragedy to really bring people together. We'd been through a tragic war. My, our people were ready to work for the Lord.

Hooper: Place yourself in the period from 1945 to 1965. How do you see yourself?

Collins: My enthusiasm fitted perfectly. My goal setting and enthusiastic preaching fit in perfectly. I'd announce goals in meetings. I'd try to have evangelistic type sermons and motivate people. It was an age when it was easy to motivate. War was not the answer. They wanted to keep it from happening again. They brought their friends and they helped the preacher convert others. We baptized people. And nothing makes a church more enthusiastic than to see a little water splashing. Nothing encourages a meeting more than baptizing people. And the people would say, "Man, see the reports of how the Church of Christ is growing. See how much larger the church is." It was a positive time for goal-setting and enthusiastic preaching. And I think whatever talents I have fit in perfectly with that age.

Hooper: You were in Lipscomb in the 1930s and returned before the end of World War II. Compare the school then and during the years of growth as a senior college, as you see the school in the past and the present.

Collins: Yes, I've been at Lipscomb since 1934 when I came as a student and I've been close to it since then. I lived at Old Hickory several years but I kept in touch with it pretty well and worked in the alumni association. When I first came to Lipscomb it was a family. Today you cannot have the same family atmosphere. We knew each other. We knew each other's problems and just knew nearly all the students. You can do that when you've got a two-year college, with a senior class of under one hundred.

When World War II came the school just didn't have many students. The college was down to nearly nothing. We might have had five hundred total, kindergarten through college. After the war these veterans returned, and the girls returned and it grew, grew. The school was growing and we were enthusiastic. The faculty was growing, everybody was enthusiastic about the school.

The future looked wonderful. Lipscomb reached two plateaus, the first was back in the '50s and then another one in the '60s.

I never will forget the decision. We had a motto, "a better, not a bigger Lipscomb."

We finally decided to change in the '60s and we got the government to build the Science Building, Fanning Hall, and the Dining Center. We had to do something. It was crowded, since we decided to go on up to twenty-two or three hundred students from fourteen hundred fifty. We changed that motto and borrowed government funds from the Johnson administration.

Now we have all these buildings—High Rise, third floor of Fanning, the Dining Center, and the Science Building. It was tremendous. We just about built a new campus. We've done more good; we've encouraged more students. But we have lost the family tie. You can't be a family with 2,200 students.

Today, we do not have the control of the students as in the 1930s. When I was in school at Lipscomb and had a date on Saturday night, all the couples would get together, get on the same bus and a chaperone would take us to town. In the age of the automobile you can't keep the family spirit. In the age of bigness you can't remain a family.

When I was in school here, only two boarding students had cars the first year. I still know their names. Now it seems that everybody's got two cars. Now we have a mobile society. Nashville's bigger. We've got more things to do.

When I was in school, the administration knew where the girls were and knew where the boys were pretty much. Or at least they thought they did. We can't have the same control of a campus of 2,200 in an automobile age that we had when I was here in the thirties.

So we try to put the right teachers and the right companions with the students. We try to get them in at a decent hour. And we try to control them the best we can. But we still have Bible every day, which I think is wonderful. We still have Christian teachers. We still have an environment that lifts up morality and lifts up God in every classroom, lifts up Christ. We still have about ninety percent members of the church and it's still a wonderful place. Lipscomb is so different from the average university or college; so different from life in downtown Nashville. It is almost still a little island.

Hooper: Comparing the young people of the 1930s and the young people of the 1980s, is there any major difference?

Collins: They're better. I really think most of them are better. I went through that age. We were not a godly bunch. In a sense we were, but when I hear some of these older preachers talk about all of the tricks and stuff they played in the dormitory, I realize they were no better than young people today.

I think today's young people think more about studying. They want to have a career. They know in this age of computers, this age of high tech, it's going to take more to compete. I really feel like most of them want to study more. A boy or girl wants to go into medicine, they knows what's ahead of them. And they're studying more. Certainly, we have a fringe of, maybe out of 100%, a fringe of one percent who cause trouble.

I think some of them may be a little less serious about going to church, and yet I was pleased with our last survey which indicated a large percentage of students attending worship. I think our students today cannot be fooled by hypocrisy as much as they could in the '30s. Man, when I came to Lipscomb I thought church was wonderful and everybody just tremendous.

Young people know more today. They know more about sexuality, know more about more things when they come to college. You can't fool them as easily today and I'm glad you can't.

I still think many of them love the church. I doubt if it's the same percentage who see the distinctiveness between the church and protestantism as students did when I came up. I doubt if we've pushed the restoration ideal as much with this generation as we have with others. I'm talking about in the past twenty-five years. I don't think they see the glory of the church, unencumbered by denominationalism, as I did when I came. I saw that when I was growing up.

Foy E. Wallace and those fellows made me feel like the church was tremendous, just wonderful. They emphasized a unified, world-wide body, a unified kingdom that will never be destroyed.

Hooper: What do you see as Lipscomb's role in today's society?

Collins: If there's a place for Lipscomb, it is to help Christian parents make stronger and better Christians. When they've gone through Lipscomb, will they be better, truer Christians by having come?

If you send a thousand young people through Lipscomb, send another thousand through state universities and colleges, I believe you'll have a greater percentage of better, truer Christians out of the thousand at Lipscomb than out of the thousand who didn't go to a Christian school. If that isn't true, this school will ultimately fail. This is the acid test it seems to me.

So if we can make engineers just as fine as anybody else, if we can give a pre-med program just as fine or a little better than big universities, that'd be great. But it's just like one of our board members said at the last meeting: "I sent my children to Lipscomb because it's a Christian school, to help them to be better Christians. That's why I paid extra money. I don't care whether you call Lipscomb a university or college or what not, I want it to be Christian. And if it's Christian, I don't care what you call it."

Hooper: Compare and contrast your role as an evangelist during the 1950s through the 1960s, and then in the last ten years.

Collins: The last ten years, we've lost something. I noticed the change in '72, '73, '74. In a period of about three years, meetings changed. We lost the revival spirit; we lost the outreach program.

People in the 1950s and 1960s were interested in growing and in bringing their neighbors to hear the gospel. They felt like the gospel was a healing message for the world and a message of hope. They believed that the world was struggling for something after World War II. And they really believed; they believed that Christ and God were the answer.

Today, very few members of the average congregation even want to attend a meeting during the week nights. Well they've got great programs at home on color TV. They've got entertainment centers at home. That's not all bad. It's a place where the parents can keep the children all together. Widows don't want to get out at night, many of them are afraid to.

The average congregation has two or three night programs going every week. By the time you go to church two or three nights a week at your home congregation you're not very enthusiastic about going to somebody else's church.

In the 1940s and 1950s, meetings were combined with seeing people. Christians enjoyed being with each other. But now they see each other regularly in their home congregation. Each congregation builds up a strong unit. They no longer depend so much on other congregations.

Madison is interested in Madison, and Hillsboro is interested in Hillsboro, and Crieve Hall interested in Crieve Hall. I think organized ball teams have a tremendous effect on attendance. That's a good thing. I can't be opposed if the community organizes a little league and they play two or three nights a week. I think it's a great thing for the community. It's a great thing to keep those kids at home. You can go up to Gladeville, Tennessee, it's the softball capital of the world, and they're going to softball games. You've got a grandchild out there playing, you want to see the grandchild. You've got a little boy out there playing, you go see the boy. When you put them all together: color TV, full-fledged local congregatons, organized sports, you just have a hard time getting people to come to meetings. They just come because they feel obligated and they don't feel obligated to bring other people.

Hooper: You aren't baptizing as many people in meetings now as in the past. Why is that true?

Collins: We don't have the outsiders; prospects are not present I can hold a meeting now and have two prospects, maybe three or four, come on a regular basis. They're mostly young people. A meeting is good to revive some members of the church, but it has lost it's power in most places with an outreach program to the unbaptized. Unless we can get the members to take time to bring their friends who are not members of the church, conversions will be fewer in number.

Hooper: Why are there not as many young men going into preaching in the 1980s as in the 1940s and the 1950s?

Collins: Their parents do not encourage preaching. A lot of preachers won't take the time to have boys' classes. Many preachers are too busy playing golf. Now I hate to say it, but I think the average preacher spends a lot more time in recreation than I spent while at Old Hickory.

Hooper: Are all the Christian colleges down in the number of preacher students?

Collins: All that I have checked on. Of course, there are several going into the preacher training schools. These schools reach, in a sense, a different class of older people. But yes, all that I've checked on are down. Last time I talked to Harold Hazelip at Harding Graduate School they were down from 274, I believe, to 220 students. I think one reason is the lack of security. Preachers, they don't have the security funds and pension funds that others have. Yet I didn't think much about that when I started preaching.

Hooper: Why do many preachers who have preached for a long time get out of regular preaching?

Collins: They see the end to their preaching coming when they'll be sixty and sixty-five. Nobody wants them and they hate to face it. Therefore, they quit preaching in their late forties or early fifties.

Hooper: From every indicator, churches of Christ are not growing as rapidly now as in the 1950s and the 1960s. Why?

Collins: First, I don't think members of the church believe the church is different from protestantism. When I started preaching, members of the church believed protestants needed to be saved. We've lost a lot of that. It goes back to an understanding of the distinctiveness of the church. At an earlier time they really felt the gospel was a lot better than protestantism. Why are the Mormons growing? They're the fastest growing religious group in this country. They're out door-to-door, in spite of apartments and other discouragements. They're still out and they're growing. That's discouraging to me.

Next, in my opinion, so many in the church of Christ have lost their caring spirit, for each other and for the lost. We're so wrapped up in our families and so wrapped up in our businesses, we don't have time for others. I don't believe the average member of the church cares as much for his neighbor and the lost as we did when I was a boy. Maybe that's because I'm older. But somehow we have lost our caring spirit.

Somebody told me the other day that the church of Christ is the only army that shoots its wounded. A member of the church stops coming, do many elders care any more whether they come or go? I mean I know they care but I don't find many congregations that have any kind of real active program. If somebody stops coming, they may not know about it for several weeks. And what do they do about it? I mean, if people stop coming to church, do we care? I hope I'm wrong.

Hooper: You are a sociologist. Are the above problems more real—is it because people in churches of Christ are more middle class and even upper middle than when you started preaching?

Collins: That's part of it. Old Hickory was a working class people. I see people with more money now. Young married couples are making more money when they first get started than teachers make at Lipscomb.

Money makes us feel a little more self-sufficient as you know. We are rich in this country. We are richer than ninety-five percent of the people in the world, I understand. That is not conducive to real Christianity. And yet it should be. We should be thankful. But we've lost that caring spirit.

Hooper: What must churches do to regain the growth of past decades?

Collins: I don't know how much humanism has affected people. But I think we've got to come back to the fact that the soul is very important. I never hear people talk about going to hell any more.

Nor do I hear anybody talking about being lost. We must get back to the fact that we are souls and we've got to go to eternity somewhere and there are only two places to go, heaven and hell. We must love people as souls and love the God who gave us Christ enough to do something about it. If we don't love enough to do something about the lost I don't know what the future will be.

Hooper: And, of course, there isn't much preaching about heaven because we have everything here.

Collins: Who wants to go? Americans have beautiful homes with air conditioning. It's great. We live in a great country. I imagine the people of Ethiopia would be more interested in heaven. Why, we're just so happy here, we want to stay and heaven doesn't mean as much as it used to.

Hooper: What do you see for churches of Christ in the near future? In the twenty-first century?

Collins: I'm hoping there's going to be a turn. There'll ultimately be a revival. We'll have to reach the place in this country I guess where we can say, "My, we can't go on like this. We're going to tear ourselves apart. We're going to steal ourselves to death."

So many people are committing adultery. We're going to get in such turmoil that somebody, two or three leaders, are going to have to come to say, "Let's go back." And I believe that time is getting nearer. I feel that the nineties, toward the close of the century, we're going to have a turn. I really feel like there's going to be a turn.

Hooper: You have spent much of your life at Lipscomb. What do you want Lipscomb to become?

Collins: I'd like for Lipscomb to become a Christian university with about 2,500 or 2,700 students. Lipscomb should become a university only when it arrives as a fine college.

First, I want it to become a fine college offering three or four master's degrees. Only then should different schools be established. Then the schools become colleges. If Lipscomb should become a Christian university, with at least four or five colleges under it, I hope one of them is a college of Biblical studies.

Hooper: What are your plans for retirement?

Collins: I haven't made any specific plans. I'll still preach some when I retire. I hope I can stay at Lipscomb in some capacity to help raise money. And to give whatever good influence I have for Lipscomb.

We have had so many disappointments in changing presidents. I hope this can be one where I can give my influence to the school and, for a while at least, acquaint the new president with the best donors. I want to continue to help raise money to keep this thing going. I'd like to help finish this endowment of thirty million dollars. And then help set a goal for more millions.

But I do hope I can give whatever influence I have in the church to Lipscomb on a permanent basis. Where the people can say, "Brother Collins is still for it and he's still working for it and we'll help him."

Hooper: As you look back over your years of work, what are the four or five most important accomplishments that you see that you have done?

Collins: First, I would say, by helping men who wanted to become preachers. And second, I think evangelism. They say I've had a little part in helping lead nearly 7,000 people to be baptized into Christ. Third, at Lipscomb I appreciate having helped build a Christian college. I think that's something for all the future.

And then fourth, the development of the Burton property to help sustain Lipscomb. And I would say number five is starting the thirty million dollar endowment program. I don't see it right now, but maybe in the future having starting the graduate program will be one of the big accomplishments. Right now it looks small. But starting to give the M.A. degree in Bible may be the beginning of a lot of graduate programs.

Hooper: You had great success at Old Hickory. Have you ever thought that maybe you should have remained in local preaching?

Collins: No. If I had it to do over again, I would still come to Lipscomb.

I think I've done more good in having chances to be with young people in chapel and encourage them and go out than I would if I'd just been local work. No, I, with my talents, whatever they may be, with my nature, I think I've done more good by coming and combining preaching and administrative work at Lipscomb.

Hooper: About your work as a Bible teacher, you mentioned the other day that probably the most enjoyable period of your time at Lipscomb was when you were teaching and working with chapel.

Collins: Just as far as enjoying it and having a good time, it was back in the '60s when I had a freshman class, 225-230 students. I had a paper grader, Marie Moyers. We had only one chapel then, so I'd go into that 9 o'clock class and they lifted me up. I hope I helped them a little bit. They lifted me up. Marie would grade papers. I'd put her up there in the balcony and she'd check the roll. I'd go in to the classroom and have an opening song and present the student of the day. We had a good time teaching the Bible. Then I'd go to chapel with the kids. It was a happy time.

Dr. Ira North   Batsell Barrett Baxter   James Byers

Willard Collins, Jimmy Allen and Batsell Baxter

B. C. Goodpasture

Chapter Eight

This is How I Write

Everyone agrees that it is impossible to capture Willard Collins' sermons in print. The qualities that make his sermons powerful do not translate into well-structured sentences. For instance, he repeats for emphasis. He constantly returns to a concept to make his point. Therefore an article that fails to repeat a phrase over and over cannot contain the spirit of the man who has been responsible for over 6,000 persons responding for baptism.

Attempts have been made to capture his sermons in print. The sermons of the Collins-Craig meeting were published. The series, *Great Preachers of Today*, includes a volume of his sermons. Neither volume has the sound of evangelist Collins, however.

Willard Collins' earliest articles were written for the *20th Century Christian*. Beginning in 1939, the magazine featured his articles throughout the 1940s and early in the 1950s. Many of the articles contained illustrative material often used in his sermons. These articles are nearer to Collins the speaker than anything of his in print.

* * *

REMEMBER FRANK

Picture Frank as a high school graduate, just ready to leave to enter college. His father is wealthy enough to afford a car for Frank to use in college. So far Frank has been carefully supervised, in life, by his parents in making most decisions.

Frank enters college. He meets several students and takes them riding. Soon he sees a knot swell on one of the tires. He almost makes up his mind to take it to the station and have it fixed, but he doesn't do it. Several students go riding with him. The tire blows out. The car careens into a pole. As Frank crawls out and looked at the smashed front end he replies to his fellow passengers: "I almost had that tire fixed yesterday, but just didn't do it."

Winter draws nearer. Frank knows he will need some antifreeze for the car. He almost takes the car to the garage to get all water connections examined, but he doesn't. The station attendant puts in a gallon of antifreeze. It is to last all winter. In a few days it has leaked out. As Frank watches the mechanic tighten loose connections he states, "I almost brought the car here several days ago before I got the antifreeze, but I just didn't do it. Now I'll have to have another gallon." The social season at college advances. After a party Frank is offered a drink. His parents' warning from high school days echoes, "A drunkard is not well-pleasing to God" (1 Cor. 5:11). He almost refuses to take his first drink, but his jolly companions win as he drinks.

Five weekends later Frank sobers from his third period of drunkenness. He is in a hospital with a broken arm and a ragged cheek. He remembers that his car is a wreck. On opening his eyes he remarks to the nurse, "You know I almost refused a few weeks ago to take my first drink, but I just didn't do it." About this time Frank's mother enters with the news, "Son, I have some things to talk to you about when you are better."

Remember Frank. His "almost-did it" never did do anything.

* * *

SOULS OR SAUSAGE

A Nashville minister, a few years ago, advertised the sermon subject, "Souls or Sausage." Those noticing the subject wondered what his text would be. At the proper time the minister read the text from Matt. 8:34, "And behold, the whole city came out to meet Jesus; and when they saw him, they besought him that he would depart out of their coasts." The story with the text states that when Jesus came into the country of the Gergesenes two met him possessed with devils. Jesus cast out these devils. These devils, when cast out, went into a herd of swine and the swine ran into the sea and perished in the waters. After the swine were destroyed the people of the city came and invited Jesus to leave their country. Thus the Nashville minister stressed the point that these people loved their sausage more than they loved their souls. Jesus could have saved their souls but since he had caused destruction to their hogs they were not interested in salvation from Jesus.

What think you of Christ? Is your business of more importance to you? Are you allowing sausage to keep you from being a Christian?

Jesus is God's mouthpiece to us. "God, who at sundry times and in divers manners spake in time past unto the fathers by the prophets, hath in these last days spoken unto us by his Son..." (Heb. 1:1-2). What does God require an accountable person to do to be saved from his past sins? Jesus gives the answer, "Go ye into all the world, and preach the gospel to every creature. He that believeth and is baptized shall be saved; but he that believeth not shall be damned" (Mark 16:15-16).

Christ is more important than any worldly job. According to Luke 5:27-28 Levi left his job to follow Christ. Young men and women often allow a certain job to keep them from living the Christian life. The job is not that important. Give up such a job and find one where you can be a follower of Christ. No job is important enough to cause one to be lost.

Christ is the one way to heaven. "I am the way, the truth and the life; no man cometh unto the Father, but by me" (John 14:6). Since God has but one son there is but one way to heaven. Heaven cannot be likened to a large railroad terminal with many different tracks but all leading to the same place. There is but one way to heaven and that way is Christ.

Recently a group of grown people were discussing another grown woman. This woman had heard the gospel and knew her duty. However, the mother of this lady who knew her duty was not a Christian and was prejudiced against the church. The ladies in conversation remarked that this girl might become a Christian when the mother died. Yet the Bible says, "He that loveth father or mother more than me is not worthy of me" (Matt. 10:37). If we allow mother even to keep us out of Christ we fail to put Christ first.

Many couples and sweethearts are now separated. While you are away plan to meet in Christ by reading about Him at a certain time each day and praying to God through the name of Christ after the reading. Even though 2,000 miles separate loved ones, those who are followers of Christ can unite with him over the miles and find rest. Jesus says: "Come unto me all ye that labor and are heavy laden, and I will give you rest" (Matt. 11:28).

* * *

WAR-TIME GOODBYES

Mary and Jim fell in love while they were seniors in high school. Three years later they were married. Jim was employed in the milk plant. Mary became a housewife in their new apartment. They were very happy.

A year later Jim received his classification. A few weeks more and they were spending their last day together before Jim was leaving for the army camp. The two of them loved their country but they were having long, long thoughts for they also loved each other and their home.

Mary went with him the day he left the station. Mary and Jim were brave but when they parted, the one from the other, lips were quivering and tears soon came. She went back to the apartment. He went to the army. Their friends said, "It is so sad for such a fine young couple to have to be separated." Yet the friends knew that the country was at war and that such things go with war.

Each war-time goodbye might remind Christians of Paul's message to Timothy, "This charge I commit unto thee, son Timothy, according to the prophecies which went before on thee, that thou by them mightest war a good warfare; holding faith..." (1 Tim. 1:18-19). Each war-time goodbye makes me desire to fight sin a little harder. Every war-time goodbye causes me to desire to teach more people the message of Christ. Every husband that leaves the station with tears and every lonely wife at home should serve as inspirations to all Christians to fight Satan and sin more than ever. Members of the church arise to the need of the hour! Be lifted up by the present-day sorrows and war-time goodbyes to uphold the truth and condemn the wrong.

Neither do I forget the young men of foreign birth who have never had the opportunity of hearing the gospel of Christ. They have been trained upon the selfish philosophies of dictatorships. Instead of being taught the brotherhood of man they have been encouraged to hate. The airplane, gun and submarine have been presented as their protective armor. Eternity, it seems, has been forgotten. Now as tank meets tank, as gun meets gun and as submarine meets submarine millions of these young men are buried in an early grave. I hate the sin that forces this grave upon them.

And while they die our boys die. This should cause us all the more to hate the sinful teaching that drives the enemy.

Such scenes being enacted upon the world stage ought to inspire every member of the body of Christ to do more in the post-war world to evangelize every community possible here and abroad.

What is a new car compared to a life? Too long the new car has been considered of more value than the souls of men. Would you help prevent war-time goodbyes for the next generation? Then sacrifice now that the world may be saturated with the gospel of Christ.

* * *

DEATH CAME SUDDENLY AT 29

Yesterday I was called to the Johns' home because of the sudden death of a 29-year-old son in a distant city. Upon arriving, I found several sorrowing friends had gathered in the living room to comfort, as best they could, these parents who awaited the arrival of the body of their dead son. The father had just returned from the tuberculosis sanitarium for the funeral and was in a back bedroom. I went in to talk with him.

The face of this 56-year-old man was drawn. He had been through so much trouble. For the last three years his wife had been sick and unable to be up attending to the duties of her home. For over twelve months he had been in the sanitarium making a fight against that dreaded disease. During this time his wife had been in another hospital; two boys had gone to the army; one had roved the streets seeking trouble; and other children had wandered in various cities.

Now word had been received that the 29-year-old son had been killed 480 miles away. It was an automobile accident. Circumstances connected with the death were none too favorable. He left behind a wife and two small children. But saddest of all, the boy had never been a Christian.

I shook hands with the sick, bereaved father. Tears rolled from his eyelids as he said, "How I wish I had the past 35 years to live over again. There are so many changes I would make." The clouds were low outside; it was raining, a cold April shower. Yet the clouds of sorrow were deeper in that room, as they poured out a cold story of life.

Mr. Johns was not a Christian. According to the teachings of the Bible he knew he was in a lost condition; for inspired Luke has written that salvation is only in Christ. (Acts 4:12). This father knew he had neglected his children. For this the Bible holds him accountable: "Fathers, provoke not your children to wrath, but bring them up in the nurture and admonition of the Lord" (Eph. 6:4). Already one was dead, who had followed in his footsteps, and remained out of Christ. This boy's chance of salvation was over. The father knew he had no Savior. No wonder he wanted to live over the past 35 years. Yet he knew better than anybody that such a wish could not be granted. Yes, indeed, the clouds of despair hung heavy within that bedroom.

I left the room to make further arrangements for the funeral. The singers had a harder time selecting the songs than they would have had if the young man had been a Christian. The preacher found it hard to prepare a message with much comfort for the bereaved family gathered around the casket. Yet we all could only do our best.

Today we had the funeral—songs were sung, prayers were said; yet there was not any evident hope for eternal life in the service. The body was carried to the cemetery. The grave was banked with flowers, and then we had the dismissal. I walked from the grave to the car with the mother. As we walked she sobbed and said, "This is so hard on me in more ways than one." I knew what she meant, for Mrs. Johns knew the teachings of the New Testament. She got into the car, closed the door, and soon the car was lost in the distance.

I then climbed into another car and drove from the cemetery. As the car rolled along I thought of how badly all young people from 15 to 27, who may have their 35 years yet to live, need teaching and encouragement to live these years in Christ and in the church. As the wheels rolled over the pavement I thought of the many young people who may have to face sudden death at 29 and who are now unprepared to meet it. I thought of such young people who might be spared until they were 56 and who then would want to live it over again. I rode on, determined to keep this from happening in as many families as I could.

* * *

DETERMINATION TO CARRY ON

Joe Sanders, six feet two inches tall, walked up to the ticket window in Columbia, Tennessee, in April and ordered a round-trip ticket to Pasquo, Washington. The ticket agent looked up and recognized the tall, blond, young man as the local evangelist and wondered, no doubt, why he was planning to make a trip of over 5,000 miles.

This young man of twenty-eight had been invited to travel over 5,000 miles to preach in a two-weeks meeting by a congregation who knew him and had heard him preach the gospel. But this ticket agent did not know the trials and hardships experienced by this young man as he had prepared to preach.

Sixteen months before Joe Sanders had moved to Columbia to work with the Highland Avenue congregation. When he first arrived the Sunday morning Bible school attendance was approximately one hundred ten and the contribution had averaged $93 per week the previous year. Now, sixteen months later, the contribution was between $250 and $330 several weeks and it was averaging $230. Two hundred eighty-seven had attended Bible classes the Sunday before he ordered his railroad ticket. However the people of Columbia did not know of his more trying days.

He attended David Lipscomb College for two years before he moved toColumbia. There the students selected him as president of the freshman class, president of the student body, and president of the debate club. He won the Founder's Day Oratorical Contest while he was a freshman. Yet the students did not know that his wife was in the hospital fighting to regain her health and that his two boys were in McMinnville with their grandmother.

In June, 1939, Joe preached his first sermon at Nonaville, Tennessee. From that time on people began to urge him to give up his work at Dupont in Old Hickory, go to school, and give his life to the preaching of the gospel. But Joe had a family and he did not know of a means of support for them if he gave up his job and started to school. Besides in 1940 his wife was carried to the hospital with an infected lung. This was another obstacle to overcome. However, Joe did not give up. He continued to preach irregularly and to attend a men's training class at the Old Hickory Church of Christ.

On May 16, 1941, he engaged in a debate at the Charlotte Avenue church building in Nashville, Tennessee. Two young men from the training class of Charlotte Avenue and two young men from a like class in Old Hickory engaged in this discussion. Brethren Athens Clay Pullias and B. C. Goodpasture were so impressed with his ability that immediately they began to urge him to give up his job and to go to school. But Joe had a sick wife, two boys, and eight years of service with the Dupont Company. However he was willing if there was a way.

A few months later the Old Hickory congregation promised Joe

$100 per month if he would give up his job and go to school. He was making over twice this amount with Dupont. However, after eight years of service, with a sick wife and a family of two boys, he gave up that job and moved to Nashville where he started to Lipscomb. Even though he was elected to many honors he had a financial struggle.

One Sunday in the spring of 1943 he was scheduled to preach in Columbia. His wife was at home, confined to her bed, and a housekeeper and two boys were depending upon Joe Sanders. He only had two dollars and the next check from Old Hickory was not due for two weeks. He paid one dollar for gasoline, dropped the other dollar in the contribution for the Lord's work, and with determination to carry on, marched to the front of the building to meet the members following the service. Not a person present knew of his condition. However, a man passing from the church building placed a bill in his hand as he shook it. Joe found out after the people had gone home that it was a twenty-dollar bill.

He was to graduate from David Lipscomb College in June of 1943. As class orator he was happy. Yet his wife had to be carried back to the hospital and once again his family was scattered. He never faltered. He went ahead with determination. Following his graduation he was invited to preach six months in Old Hickory. During this time his wife was to be operated on three times. Joe went to the hospital early that morning for the operation. After the operation he left to preach in Old Hickory, realizing that his wife was at the point of death. He preached under that strain but he believed in prayer. After the sermon he returned to the hospital wondering if his wife would be alive. She was alive.

Those operations were successful. Week by week Mrs. Sanders became better. They have now been living together in Columbia for sixteen months. This family circle is happy because the parents and children know what it means to live apart. But the ticket agent in Columbia could not know of all these trials which the tall blond had faced when he requested the ticket to Pasquo, Washington.

When Brother Joe Willis baptized a 14-year-old boy in a mountain creek of Warren County, Tennessee, nearly fifteen years ago, he did not know that this boy would be invited across the nation to preach the gospel before he was 30. When Sister C. J. Garner taught the little blond boy in a Bible class many years ago she did not know that she was helping to train an able gospel preacher who would have such determination to carry on in the face of difficulty.

* * *

During the 1950s and the 1960s, Collins wrote numerous articles for the *Gospel Advocate*. Closely associated with the paper's editor, B. C. Goodpasture, Collins, along with Batsell Barrett Baxter and Ira North, served on a special committee to extend the circulation of the *Advocate* for its centennial year in 1955. All three men became much more visible through the pages of the journal. Beginning in 1950, Collins wrote weekly articles for the Nashville *Banner* under the title "Daily Living with Christ." The articles in both papers represent well the positive attitude that has always characterized Willard Collins.

This section of the chapter is designed to allow Collins to present his own ideas through excerpts from several of his articles from both papers.

The Nashville *Banner* was his method of sharing his ideas with a large public from February 1950 to February 1951. In the introduction to the collected articles, Charles Moss, Executive Editor of the *Banner*, stated:

> We are happy to have him [Willard Collins] incorporate into this volume the columns which have meant so much to our readers. We are humbly proud to know that our newspaper has been one channel by which Willard's great message has gone out to the world. He who reaches for this little book will hold in his hands a treasure of truth and faith and hope based on the teachings of Jesus Christ.

The following articles are from *Daily Living with Christ*.

* * *

PERMANENT SECURITY NOT GUARANTEED IN THIS WORLD

The material things of this world can never guarantee permanent security, according to Jesus who said, "Lay not up for yourselves treasures upon earth where moth and rust doth corrupt and where thieves break through and steal" (Matthew 6:19).

Christ advised His followers against the folly of trusting in this world's possessions by describing the rich fool. This man's farm brought forth much fruit in harvest. In planning future storage of this abundant crop he forgot the poor and said, "This will I do:

I will pull down my barns, and build greater; and there will I store all of my fruits and my goods" (Luke 12:18).

This individual believed his future was secure. He said, "Soul thou hast much goods laid up for many years; take thine ease, eat, drink, and be merry" (Luke 12:19). However, Jehovah taught him how insecure he really was by trusting in material treasures and said to him, "Thou fool, this night thy soul shall be required of thee: then whose shall those things be, which thou has provided?" (Luke 12:20).

Such is the fate of a man who thought he could guarantee his future by heaping together material possessions. He spent his entire life in this task and when he thought he had security, he discovered he had made no preparation for real peace at all. A man's soul cannot be fed upon the crops raised in a field.

Christians find security, not in the things of this world, but in Christ. When disaster comes their souls will be fixed in the Rock of Ages. The explosion of bombs can destroy buildings and possessions, but they cannot take away God's reward for his faithful children.

* * *

THE GOSPEL OF LOVE

The gospel of Christ has great drawing power, particularly as is evidenced in the conversion of Saul of Tarsus, who is best known as the apostle Paul.

After Paul became submissive to Christ, he said, "For I am not ashamed of the gospel: for it is the power of God unto salvation to everyone that believeth; to the Jew first, and also to the Greek" (Romans 1:16). What are the attractive features in this message delivered by the Savior?

The Power of Love

Love is one of the appealing characteristics of the doctrine of Christ. Love binds a mother to her child, a husband to his wife, and a child to its parents. Without love the oration is ineffective and the death of the martyr is unavailing. Paul taught this when he wrote, "Though I speak with the tongues of men and of angels, and have not love, I am become sounding brass, or a clanging cymbal...and if I give my body to be burned, but have not love, it profiteth me nothing" (I Corinthians 13:1 and 3).

132

Directions of Love

Man's love should first be turned toward God. When Christ was asked which commandment was the greatest, he replied, "Thou shalt love the Lord thy God with all thy heart, and with all thy soul, and with all thy mind, and with all thy strength" (Mark 12:30).

If an individual loves God with his feeling power, thinking ability, and his physical strength, this will lead him to obey God. John said, "For this is the love of God, that we keep His commandments" (I John 5:3). Love is a basic motivation which causes the creature to obey his creator.

The Christian must also direct his love toward his neighbor. When He gave the second commandment Christ said, "Thou shalt love thy neighbor as thyself" (Mark 12:31). Love for a neighbor will enable the disciple of Jesus to practice the golden rule—'And as you would that men should do to you, do ye also unto them likewise" (Luke 6:31). This guide of conduct for life's relationships will prevent stealing, murder, gossip, lying, and all other such sins so habitually practiced.

Love is so prevalent in the gospel of Christ that it unites brethren in the church and prompts the followers of Christ to seek and attempt to save lost souls. For example, young men from four different parts of the world conducted services at the Charlotte Avenue Church of Christ in Nashville one Sunday evening. Neil Lawrence, Hawaii, led the song service; Shegeji Kogachi, Hawaii, read the Scripture lesson; and Dieter Goebbel, Frankfurt, Germany, led the prayer. After the prayer Ralph Perry, Ontario, Canada, Fred Casmir, Frankfurt, Germany, and Hugh Tinsley, Belfast, Ireland, told of the influences of the gospel in their native lands. These young men who live thousands of miles apart have been united by Christ's message of love.

Jesus came to this world "to save sinners" (1 Timothy 1:15). Soldiers of the cross must have this spirit of Christ which led the disciples in Jerusalem over 1,900 years ago to go "about preaching the word" (Acts 8:4).

* * *

WHAT JESUS CAN MEAN TO YOU

Jesus Christ can mean more to an individual in daily living than any other character. Quite often I like to personally consider the question, "What does Jesus mean to me?"

The activities of everyday life have become so numerous that it is difficult to take off enough time to consider the question, "What does Jesus mean to me?" Yet our lives could be richer in content if we would let Jesus dwell in our hearts through faith.

Jesus, the Light To Your Path

Jesus can brighten your pathway in life. He said, "I am the light of the world: he that followeth me shall not walk in the darkness, but shall have the light of life" (John 8:12).

As long as a person stands in the sunlight with his back to the sun, his shadow will be in front of him. Every time he takes a step, the shadow takes a corresponding step. Just as long as the individual's back is to the sun, the shadow is in his pathway. The shadow can be removed from the pathway only when the person faces the sun. The path of life is always filled with sunlight when the traveler faces the sun.

Jesus is the best answer to trouble, sorrow and death because Jesus is the Son of Righteousness. When trouble and sorrow have shaded your pathway, remember to turn your face toward Christ and your shadow will get behind you. Paul taught this lesson when he wrote "And we know to them that love God all things work together for good, even to them that are called according to His purpose" (Romans 8:28).

It is impossible to live in this world without experiencing sorrow, trouble and disappointments. However, the one who is following Christ day by day is better prepared to face such experiences because Christ is a source of strength and light for a troubled soul.

Jesus, the Savior of Your Soul

Man is a living soul by creation of God. H. Leo Boles, a former president of David Lipscomb College who trained over 1,500 young men to preach Christ, stressed this fact to his students. Man is not a physical body—man is a soul and he has a body as a temporary house. Moses wrote, "And Jehovah God formed man of the dust of the ground, and breathed into his nostrils the breath of life; and man became a living soul" (Genesis 2:7).

Life is made up of hours, days, months and years. As you experience these different time intervals, take Christ with you as your daily companion. Christ can be the light to your pathway and the savior of your soul. Man as a living soul is of too much value to be enslaved by Communism or the totalitarian state. The human being is of too much worth to spend his life as a servant of sin.

* * *

HOPE OF IMMORTALITY

Job asked a question which has disturbed mankind for centuries when he wrote, "If a man die, shall he live again?" (Job 14:14).

Some have discussed immortality in terms of the continuance of the race and the endurance of mental and moral qualities. Others have discussed this subject as it might relate to influence and memory, but Job has asked about the hope of the individual to live beyond the grave.

The Story of a Friend

Harold Hays and I were boyhood pals. We played together, hunted, and attended school together for years in Lewisburg, Tennessee. Both of us went to Sunday school and church regularly, but after graduation from high school in 1934, we were separated.

During the period of World War II, Harold became a pilot. One afternoon in North Carolina his plane crashed and he was killed. His body was returned to the cemetery on his grandfather's farm near Lewisburg for burial. When I visited Harold's grave, I saw the woods where we hunted, the fields where we used to play, and the pathways we had known so well. As I read the marker on the grave, I knew that we could never do these things again.

However, if my childhood friend continued faithfully in Christ until his death and if I will strive faithfully until my life is over, I have the hope of reunion. I do not know too much about it and I will leave details in the hands of God.

This is the hope that spurs a Christian on when he buries his faithful loved one. The resurrection of Christ declares that man shall live again. Fear of the atom and hydrogen bombs cannot destroy this hope.

* * *

From 1944 onward, Willard Collins' name appeared regularly in the columns of the *Gospel Advocate*. Most often, however, it was relative to his work at David Lipscomb College, either as assistant Director of the Lipscomb Expansion Program or as vice president of the school. In 1955, he was selected, along with Batsell Barrett Baxter and Alan Bryan, as the Centennial Committee to increase the circulation of the Advocate. From that time forward Collins began to appear as a writer for the *Advocate* and the editor of a small column "That's a Good Idea." His topics were varied, often dealing with current concerns.

* * *.

Television was relatively new in 1955. But already concern was being voiced about this new medium. Willard Collins in the following article indicates the decisions facing parents as they direct their children toward adulthood.

THE IMPACT OF TELEVISION UPON SOCIETY

One hundred years ago, the average American family huddled around the candle and the book. In the 1950's, the family of this nation enjoys the fluorescent lamp and the television set. Think of the change in one hundred years.

Broadcasting and telecasting are by far children's favorite means of entertainment in this generation. Based upon one hundred per cent, they list broadcasting and telecasting at 87.5. Books drop to 18.5; movies, to 4.5; and comics drop to one per cent. This shows the tremendous impact that television is having upon the family.

WHAT ARE SOME OBLIGATIONS OF CHRISTIAN PARENTS IN CONNECTION WITH THIS MEDIUM?

There are two great obligations that Christian parents and teachers owe to the children and young people of this nation in connection with television. They must be trained to become discriminating viewers, and television must be used not only for entertainment, but also as a medium of education.

Television is here and will remain. Most families are going to watch it. Christian people should take the lead in using this medium in the right way. This means discriminating in viewing, developing proper taste in regard to programs watched, and seeking ways of using this medium as a means of education as well as entertainment.

A part of the training which Christian parents could give their children is this development of good taste in the selection of books, magazines, and radio programs, as well as television. The television screen opens a window on the world in the living rooms of our homes. With proper discrimination, there are times when the shade will be drawn over the window.

IS DEVELOPING THE PROPER ATTITUDE TOWARD EVIL A FUN-
DAMENTAL JOB OF PARENTS?

The developing of the ability to choose between right and wrong
in one of the most fundamental jobs of Christian parents in the
training of their children. Paul stated the principle in these words:
"Abhor that which is evil; cleave to that which is good" (Rom. 12:9).

The ideal is that young people be trained in order that they may
do the things they love to do without doing the things which are
wrong. It is no wonder that Jesus stressed the importance of appetite in the sermon on the mount.

When this proper appetite is developed, individuals can make
the proper decisions concerning television programs and any other
problem they face in today's world.

* * *

The greatest influence on Willard Collins' early life was his
mother, Maxie Collins. She provided the opportunities for her son
to develop those qualities necessary for making Collins an outstanding evangelist. About six and a half months before his mother's
death, he wrote the following tribute to mother.

* * *

ENDLESS LOVE OF MOTHER

Intense suffering did not cause Jesus to forget the welfare of his
mother, because from the cross he said to one of his apostles,
"Behold, thy mother."

John, in describing the scene where Jesus asked him to take care
of Mary, said, "When Jesus therefore saw his mother, and the disciple standing by whom he loved, he saith unto his mother, Woman,
behold, thy son! Then saith he to the disciple, Behold, thy mother!
And from that hour the disciple took her unto his own home" (John
19:26, 27).

IMPORTANCE OF TRAINING

Christ recognized the value of training given to children by their
mothers. Paul, one of his apostles, wrote, "I desire therefore that
the younger women marry, bear children, rule the household, give
no occasion to the adversary for reviling" (1 Tim. 5:14).

In describing woman's work, Paul wrote to Titus that the aged
women should train the young women to "love their husbands,
to love their children, to be sober-minded, chaste, workers at home,

137

kind, in subjection to their own husbands" (Tit. 2: 4, 5).

A young lady may type but the typewritten page will fade; and she may make shoes but the shoes will wear out, but when the young woman marries and becomes a mother, she shapes a treasure not just for this world but for the existence to come.

I have admired the beautiful Lincoln Memorial in Washington, D. C., on several occasions. It is marvelous that human hands could carve such a resemblance, but there is a log cabin in Kentucky where the real Lincoln was born. A mother began shaping a character in the log cabin that finally became a great president. Thus we admire the woman who helped carve the real Lincoln more than the person who chiseled and polished the imitation now displayed in the nation's capital.

Architects of enormous skyscrapers and engineers of great bridges are justly esteemed but may we never forget the nation's mothers who are God's builders of men.

* * *

From earliest preaching days, Willard Collins emphasized the family. Most meetings included at least one sermon on the family and the home. And certainly his interest in the home reflects what he considered to be important in the Collins' home.

THE ONE-PARENT HOME

Seven million children under eighteen years of age are now living in one-parent homes in this Nation.

These homes have been made incomplete either by divorce, separation, or death.

In each case, there is a struggling parent who is trying to carry on in the place of both parents. Loneliness is often a characteristic of the one-parent home.

Parents in a Christian family should realize how fortunate they are. The companionship of a Christian husband and wife may be the nearest place to heaven on earth.

GOD'S PLAN OF MARRIAGE

The same God who gave us the scheme of redemption also gave man a plan of marriage. Since God made man and knows what it takes for man to be happy, then this picture of marriage from God is the best way devised for man.

God's plan of marriage as given through Christ states "And he answered and said unto them, Have ye not read, that he which made them at the beginning made them male and female, And said, For this cause shall a man leave father and mother, and shall cleave to his wife: and they twain shall be one flesh? Wherefore they are no more twain, but one flesh. What therefore God hath joined together, let not man put asunder" (Matt. 19: 4, 5, 6).

From this passage one notices that it is God's way for one man and one woman to become one and to live together in love and faithfulness to each other until death. Children can come into this situation to be trained for Christ and heavens.

* * *

Preaching has been Willard Collins' life. Whether at Old Hickory, Charlotte Avenue, or David Lipscomb College, he has encouraged young men to preach. The following excerpt indicates Collins' Interest in preaching.

GREAT PREACHING AND GREAT TRUTH

Truth makes men free.

A knowledge of the truth is essential before men can be made free by it.

Disciples of Christ as they continue in the word are the ones who are guaranteed a knowledge of the truth.

Jesus gave this truth to the Jews who believed on him: "If ye continue in my word, then are ye my disciples indeed; and ye shall know the truth, and the truth shall make you free" (John 8:31,32).

Who is a Christian? The gospel teaches that a Christian is a disciple, "And the disciples were called Christians first at Antioch" (Acts 11:26). A disciple of Christ is one who continues to abide in his word. Jesus gave this specific promise when he said: "If ye continue in my word, then are ye my disciples indeed" (John 8:31). There is an everlasting connection between truth and being a Christian.

THE VALUE OF PREACHING

Preaching is God's way of making the great truth known: "For after that in the wisdom of God the world by wisdom knew not God, it pleased God by the foolishness of preaching to save them that believe" (1 Cor. 1:21).

Chapter Nine

Friends Closer Than Brothers

Friendship is characteristic of Willard Collins. Literally thousands of people around the world consider Willard Collins as a friend. There are few, if any, acquaintances who are not his friend. In any discussion of a town or city where he has held meetings, he can recall a person or persons who hold some special place in his memory. Those persons are his friends.

As always, though, there have been a few men who have been close friends. These men have known him in his very private moments when he needed someone to share his innermost feelings. One person, Franklin Camp, has been a friend since college days. In 1986, he remains Collins' closest confidant.

Others who have shared a special friendship with Collins are now dead—James Byers, B. C. Goodpasture, Batsell Barrett Baxter, and Ira North. With the passing of Byers and Goodpasture, a very close relationship became even closer with Baxter and North. Truly, there are "friends who stick closer than a brother."

* * *

Moving to Nashville in 1960 from Chattanooga, the James Byerses lived on Gateway Lane, only a short distance from the Collinses' home on Lealand Lane. Byers became a member of Lipscomb's Board of Directors on October 15, 1943. At that time, he was owner of Stovall Hardware in Chattanooga and a number of other businesses including fabric shops, in Chattanooga and Atlanta. These he owned jointly with Leslie Self of Nashville. Nashville and Lipscomb offered the opportunities for Christian education unavailable to their children in Chattanooga.

Byers was a graduate of Lipscomb in 1927 when it was a junior college. Here he met his future wife, Ruth Tracey of Sistersville, West Virginia. Before marriage and returning to Chattanooga, Byers earned his degree from the University of Tennessee in Knoxville. His parents had died early in life. Oscar Crisman, then owner of Stovall Hardware, provided guidance for young Byers and welcomed him into the family business when he finished the University.

The St. Elmo church in Chattanooga was the home congregation of the Crismans and Byerses. It was here that Byers and Collins first met when the young preacher filled an occasional monthly appointment during the 1930s. Even though Byers became a member of the board in 1943, the close friendship blossomed after 1960. Personal characteristics of each man attracted the other. Mrs. Byers states that Collins never said anything ugly about anyone. Furthermore, he has always been completely trustworthy. Equally complimentary, Collins says of his friend: "Jim was a man you could trust."

Therefore, the two-mile strolls the two couples took when Collins was not away in meetings were times when Lipscomb was the center of discussion. On that somber November day in 1963 when both President Kennedy and Maxie Collins died, James and Ruth Byers were the ones the Collinses turned to in their sorrow. They accompanied them to Lewisburg to make arrangements for Collins' mother.

With the death of Harry Leathers in 1967, Byers was elected chairman of the Board of Directors. If anything, the friendship of the men deepened. The two families often traveled together. Trips were shared to Gatlinburg and Florida. On one occasion the Byerses accompanied the Collinses on a preaching engagement. Tired of waiting for the men, the women went to the Collins car. Finding the car locked, Ruth Byers tried the key to her own automobile on her friend's door. It worked. Surprised were the men when the women drove to the front of the building.

Shortly thereafter, Collins traded cars. He often told the story of Byers' keys fitting his car. He would add that he was afraid his neighbor might steal his car. Therefore, he had to trade. This was always good for a laugh between friends. James Byers was always an enthusiastic supporter of athletics at Lipscomb. The two friends and their wives were always present for Bison basketball, sharing seats halfway up on the east side of McQuiddy Gymnasium. During spring of each year, Byers was a regular at the baseball field where he urged the Bisons toward national prominence. During spring vacations, he would travel to Florida with the team. When the 1971 and 1972 teams placed second in the National Association of Intercollegiate Athletics, Byers was present. The 1974 team was one of the eight finalists at St. Joseph, Missouri. Even though he had suffered some chest pains, he decided to fly west for the tournament.

The trip was a mistake. Byers suffered an attack between Nashville and Memphis, but continued on to St. Joseph. Shortly after arrival, he died in his motel room. The baseball team was stunned; the fans could not believe "Brother Byers" was dead.

Back home in Nashville, Mrs. Byers was having dinner with her son and daughter-in-law, Jim and Marie Byers, and her grandson, Tracey. Unable to reach the Byerses because of a malfunctioning phone, a caller reached Willard and Ruth Collins. They went to the younger Byers' home to relay the news that Jim Byers had had by a heart attack. Only later did they know that he was already dead.

Thus the Collinses shared death and grief with their best friends just as the Byerses had been available for comfort to their friends over a decade earlier.

Three and one-half years later, Willard Collins became president of David Lipscomb College. The concerns both men had for the school eventually led to Collins' election to the presidency. Of all those who did not share that September day, the new president had to miss Jim Byers most. Even in 1985, letters to Ruth Byers included the phrase: "I miss Jim every day."

* * *

Willard Collins has been a friend to every member of Lipscomb's faculty since he arrived on campus in December of 1944. Many of those who came during those first years of the Pullias-Collins administration began on a first-name basis with the young administrator. Joe Sanders was a friend of longstanding from Old Hickory. Tom Whitfield was a neighbor down the street when the Collinses moved to their Lealand Lane address. Carroll Ellis has long been a friend to Willard Collins.

Yet even on the faculty, there were those who shared a closer friendship with Collins. In most instances, the relationships revolved around larger concerns than David Lipscomb College. Willard Collins has always been concerned with the church in its broadest sense, including brotherhood-wide functions such as the *Gospel Advocate*, the *20 Century Christian*, and the *Herald of Truth*. A church builder, Collins was constantly aware of growing, dynamic churches, especially the one at Madison.

B. C. Goodpasture was long a friend of the Morris family in Atlanta. When Goodpasture came to Nashville in 1939 to edit the *Gospel Advocate*, Ruth and Willard Collins were just beginning their work at Old Hickory.

The friendship was already present, but not until the 1950s did the two men become involved in special work together. The *Gospel Advocate* reached its one hundreth birthday in July 1955. Several months prior to the celebration, Goodpasture appointed Willard Collins, Alan Bryan, and Ira North to the Centennial Drive Committee. The major function of the group was to increase the circulation of the *Advocate*. The first goal of 50,000 subscribers was reached. A new goal called for 100,000 subscribers by April 1, 1956.

Willard Collins began the drive during the Lipscomb Winter Lectures in 1955. Aided by Clay Pullias, Ira North, and Batsell Barrett Baxter, the effort added over 7,000 new subscribers. A number of men, including Collins, were already members of the 100 Club—those who had sold subscriptions to a hundred people.

Soon thereafter the three men were added as staff writers for the *Advocate*. Bryan, then educational director for the Broadway church in Lubbock, Texas, edited a feature called "The Daily Guide" for family Bible study. North conducted the "Know Your Bible" family quiz, and Collins wrote a column on "Outstanding Christian Families." It was a relationship that would last until Goodpasture's death in 1977.

For the special edition of the *Gospel Advocate*, published on July 14, 1955, Willard Collins wrote the biographical article on Goodpasture. After a lengthy sketch of his life, Collins indicated his feelings for his friend:

> Christ is the Master, and B. C. Goodpasture is the servant. He is filling his life full in the Master's service. The Lord has prospered this servant abundantly in his business investments and activities also.

In these critical days for the church of our Lord, may we rejoice that B. C. Goodpasture occupies the editor's chair of the *Gospel Advocate*, that he serves as president of the entire Gospel Advocate Company, and that he is an elder in one of the largest congregations in the brotherhood, because in these positions he can do so much for Christ and his church.

At Goodpasture's death in 1977, Collins penned a short article in the special edition of the *Advocate*:

B. C. Goodpasture
Was Gentle and Kind

Batsell Barrett Baxter, Ira North and I had a special relationship with B. C. Goodpasture as members of the *Advocate's* Second Century Committee. We have enjoyed many lunches together since 1955.

We laughed at his favorite stories, enjoyed his vivid memories of the past and appreciated his deep love and concern for the church.

He had a keen sense of humor and as one who knew him well for over forty-two years, I appreciated his kindness, gentleness, and genuineness.

The full impact of his death has not been comprehended. There is a big vacant chair in Nashville, Tennessee.

I feel a personal loss in not being able to call B. C. Goodpasture when I need to talk with him about some decision I must make. His advice was priceless to me. Through the years he has helped far more than he knew, in building and preserving David Lipscomb College.

Four months later, Collins would become President of David Lipscomb College.

Soon after his graduation, Goodpasture's son, Cliett, became an employee of David Lipscomb College in the Department of Bible. Serving in various capacities throughout the years, Collins chose him to be Vice President for Business Affairs in 1983. A friendship begun with the father was now complete in the son.

* * *

Responding to W. A. Reed, the religious news editor of the *Tennessean*, the day after Batsell Barrett Baxter's death on March 31, 1982, Willard Collins remarked: "I do not think of Dr. Baxter as just a national figure on radio and television but as a warm-hearted, gentle and kind person." Collins added, "As a preacher, professor and scholar, Dr. Baxter reached the summit. He was a source of strength and helped me in my work as president of David Lipscomb College. We worked together like brothers in the flesh."

Baxter and Collins had never met until 1945 when Baxter joined the Lipscomb faculty as chairman of the Speech department. Previously, Baxter had held a meeting for the College church, but it was before Collins became a fixture on the campus.

Wanda Baxter remembers the first time she saw Willard Collins. It was in 1945 as Dr. Baxter was preparing to begin his work at the school. Baxter's father was president of Lipscomb, living in Avalon Hall on the campus. The young Baxters were staying at Avalon Hall until they could secure a house of their own. In July or August, Willard Collins appeared at the door desiring to see Dr. Baxter. Mrs. Baxter remembers Collins as "such an earnest person."

Ruth Collins remembers Batsell Barrett as a freshman at Lipscomb during 1933-1934. The elder Baxter had been president of Lipscomb, returning to Abilene for the fall term in 1934. Young Baxter continued his education at Abilene before Willard Collins enrolled at Lipscomb in 1934.

Baxter and Collins shared a great love for preaching. Both men used every opportunity afforded them to preach. Both were in great demand as proclaimers of the Word. Throughout the late 1940s on through the 1960s, two of the outstanding evangelists among churches of Christ worked and taught side by side on the Lipscomb campus. Baxter held his first city-wide meeting in Lubbock, Texas. Later Collins became the most sought-after evangelist for special campaigns.

However, it was the medium of television through which Baxter became so well known as an evangelist. His unique style was perfect for the *Herald of Truth*. When it was announced that Baxter would be the speaker, his friend Willard Collins wrote: "No better man than Batsell Barrett Baxter could have been chosen by the elders of the Highland Church of Christ in Abilene to present New Testament Christianity through the new *Herald of Truth* television series."

Even though Collins was in the midst of his greatest work as an evangelist, he said of Baxter:

> No more powerful preaching is being done by any man today than by Batsell Barrett Baxter....I am thankful for the life he is living for the Lord, for his wonderful family, for what he means to David Lipscomb College and its students, for his work at Hillsboro [church], and for this great opportunity that comes to him now to declare the full gospel of Christ to American television viewers.

This attitude was reciprocal. Neither man possessed a jealous bone in his body.

* * *

Closely associated with Willard Collins and Batsell Barrett Baxter was Ira North. In the year Ruth and Willard Collins married, young Ira, finishing his senior year in high school, married Avon Stephens. In the fall of 1939, the O. L. Norths sent their son and daughter-in-law to David Lipscomb College. It was the beginning of a great team effort in church growth.

North finished his B.A. degree at Abilene Christian, then he matriculated to Urbana, Illinois, where he received his M.A. from the University of Illinois. He returned to Nashville and David Lipscomb College where he taught until he took a leave of absence to complete his Ph.D. at Louisiana State University. He returned to Lipscomb and accepted the pulpit of the 400-member Madison Church of Christ.

North, Collins, and Baxter were quickly attracted to each other. Collins suggested that Baxter was much more like a brother than just a friend. The same relationship existed between Collins and North and Baxter and North. Possibly the three men were attracted to each other because all were only children. They did not have brothers and sisters to share their concerns and their pleasures, their problems and their victories.

At some time in 1954, Willard Collins was host to Batsell Barrett Baxter at his home on Temple Avenue. Discussion centered on some method of encouraging Bible study in Middle Tennessee. The idea for *Know Your Bible* was born with this conversation. Since both Baxter and Collins knew Louis Draughan who owned WSIX-TV, they decided to take their idea to the station owner. Draughan liked the concept. Baxter's and Collins' schedules would not allow either man to serve as host for the show or even be a regular participant. They approached Ira North about the leadership position. He quickly accepted.

The program was an immediate success, with Charles Brewer, Sara Whitten, and Charles Chumley serving as regular participants. For six consecutive years the show was judged the best religious program in Middle Tennessee. It continued until 1971 when Madison began the Amazing Grace Bible Class.

The confidence Collins exhibited toward North came from a very close relationship that began when North joined the faculty of David Lipscomb College. Equally so, North had a deep respect for Collins. On July 11, 1983, North, in a special interview concerning Collins, stated: "Willard Collins is a remarkable man. I think the key to his success over a long period of time is his genuineness. He is the same every time you see him. Willard is free from hypocrisy and sham. He is a positive person."

Willard Collins was very interested in the development of the Madison church. He watched the attendance figures climb. By 1954 they filled the 1,500 seats in the new auditorium. Two years later the church constructed a thirty-six room Sunday school annex. Soon the facilities were taxed. Madison was on its way. Ira North's enthusiasm and promotional acumen were, indeed, contagious.

Lipscomb's vice-president, an accomplished public relations person himself, joined forces with Ira North for a meeting at Madison in 1960. The facilities were strained with crowds overflowing existing auditoriums and classrooms. Already the church had a record 3,002 students in Bible classes. At the conclusion of the meeting, fifty-seven had responded for baptism and sixteen were restored. It was a great week for Madison, Willard Collins, and Ira North.

Collins challenged the congregation to do greater things in the future. Evidently having in mind the number baptized on Pentecost, he urged the elders to construct a new auditorium to seat 3,000 persons. This fit perfectly into the thinking of both Collins and North. Both have always emphasized building. Both have used goals as motivators.

A year passed before Madison moved toward Collins' suggestion. Calling their plan "Operation Forward," the elders unveiled a "Twenty-Year Development Program." The new 3,000-seat auditorium was first on the list. By 1980, they wanted two identical services with 3,000 present for each service. In 1964, the church began construction after a bond issue was oversubscribed in ten minutes. In 1965, the church held a second bond sale at the Ryman Auditorium. Because the new auditorium was modeled after the historic Ryman, the public relations impact would be enormous. It took less than eight minutes to sell the bonds. In eighteen minutes, nearly a million dollars of bonds were sold.

All of these plans and accomplishments were duly noted in the *Gospel Advocate*. The writer for each of the articles, with accompanying pictures, was Willard Collins. Two men who were premier publicists told the nation about the Madison Church of Christ, the largest congregation in the fellowship.

The building opened with Willard Collins conducting a gospel meeting. The sermons shared with the huge gatherings were typical Collins:

Love in Action
Faith in Action
Hope that Spurs Us On
Urgency of the Gospel
Seed of the Kingdom
Predicament of Modern Man
Jesus Sets the Choices Before Us
Jesus, Our Deliverer
Think What Christ Can Mean to the
Individual

It was a very successful preaching effort with thirty-three baptisms, seventeen restorations, and ten who placed membership with Madison.

* * *

Ira North was a teacher in the speech department at Lipscomb. Batsell Barrett Baxter was his immediate superior. Their relationship, however, was not employer-employee. It was as friends. The same was true when Willard Collins was a part of the trio.

Baxter joined the Centennial Committee of the *Advocate* when Alan Bryan left Lipscomb and Nashville. Soon, however, the meetings became more than an effort to extend the influence of the *Gospel Advocate*. It was a committee, when Goodpasture was present, that represented four of the most important emphases of churches of Christ. Goodpasture was editor of the most powerful journal among churches of Christ. Batsell Barrett Baxter was gaining stature as a radio speaker and would become the speaker for *Herald of Truth* radio and television. Willard Collins was the most outstanding evangelist among churches of Christ. Ira North was fast becoming the premier church builder in the fellowship.

Contrary to what some might think, the four men were not concerned with self-aggrandizement. Of the four, only Goodpasture used an occasional harsh word to counter his critics. Collins, North, and Baxter have always had the ability to follow their course without replying in kind to those who criticized their efforts. Wanda Baxter stated: "They shared the same demeanor; they would not fight back." "Nor," she added, "would they ever say anything vindictive."

Gospel Advocate committee meetings evolved into monthly luncheons for the three men. On occasion Goodpasture shared in the meetings until his death in 1977. Following 1977, the wives often were invited to attend the luncheons. After a while the three began to refer to their monthly gatherings as "Crisis" Meetings. On one Thursday, the six met at the Silver Wings restaurant at the Airport Hilton. Seated in an alcove in the rear of the restaurant, they laughed and announced that they were there to solve the problems of the brotherhood. Upon leaving, they were somewhat embarrassed to see that a group of preachers was just around the corner. Had they heard their joking pronouncement to solve all the problems of the church?

As the years passed, the comraderie increased. As an example, the Baxters determined a need for a will in the late 1950s. Since they often traveled, they decided to make some provision for their sons—Scott, Alan, and John. They asked the Collinses if they would supervise their children's rearing if something should happen to them. What greater friendship could be expressed than this!

The wives became very close friends as they looked forward to the monthly luncheons. Some of the time they engaged in conversation with the men, but most of the gatherings found them engrossed in their own special topics. At these and other social engagements, Wanda Baxter became an admirer of Ruth Collins. "Ruth's mother," said Mrs. Baxter, "taught her how to be queen in the home." She was amazed at the ease with which Mrs. Collins entertained in her home and in the President's quarters when she cooked meals for special guests. Wanda Baxter offered the greatest compliment when she noted how Mrs. Collins has stood by her husband in everything he has done.

Several years ago the Collinses purchased two double lots at Woodlawn Cemetery in Nashville. When it became obvious that the Collinses would only need one lot, they offered the other lot to the Baxters. They readily accepted. Many times Collins has told how on the Resurrection Morning he and Ruth will be with their dear friends, Batsell Barrett and Wanda Baxter.

* * *

The three good friends had a characteristic lacking in many people. They could disagree and remain as brothers. When the *Herald of Truth* began in 1952, a general swell arose across the brotherhood in support of the program. When Baxter became "the speaker to the nation," Collins wrote numerous articles in support of his friend's efforts.

Early in the 1970s, the program began to receive criticism. It did not include enough "first principles." There were questions about the operation of the program. Collins and North indicated concern. They shared their feelings with Baxter, but he felt that even with some of the problems present it remained the best possible way of reaching the millions of people where public preaching would be impossible.

With Madison continuing to grow, with Willard Collins facing major decisions and finally becoming president of Lipscomb, and with Baxter's involvement with world-wide evangelism, the monthly luncheons remained a major source of strength for the three friends who were closer than brothers.

* * *

The frailties of the human body are never limited to those who abuse themselves. Oftentimes good men and women face trials of sickness and pain. Facing the worst diagnosis of cancer, Baxter and North looked to their friends for the comfort that only friends can give.

Baxter was the first to know the illness in 1964. He called his friend Willard Collins, who was in a meeting in Beaumont, Texas, to tell him about the doctor's prognosis. Initial surgery was successful. For thirteen years Baxter continued his work at Lipscomb, Hillsboro, and with the *Herald of Truth*. In 1977, the same year Collins became president of Lipscomb, Baxter entered Vanderbilt Hospital after returning from a filming trip to the Holy Land for *Herald of Truth*. His worst fears were verified. The cancer had returned. This time it was much more extensive than before.

Few visitors were allowed, but one was urged to come. Collins spent thirty minutes with Baxter, even though the patient could speak only in a whisper. Baxter assured his friend that he was glad that Collins would be the next president of Lipscomb. In fact, he had talked earlier with a board member urging Collins' choice.

Baxter's health remained fragile for the remainder of his life. Some months prior to death, Baxter called the administrators of the college to his home. He offered to resign his positions so the school could choose a new chairman of the Bible department. The next day, however, Lipscomb's president sent word that Baxter would remain in his positions as long as he lived. Friends do not desert each other in times of trouble. On March 31, 1982, Batsell Barrett Baxter died. His death left a void in Willard Collins' life that no one could fill.

* * *

Ira North began complaining somewhat with his back in 1982. Wanda Baxter remembers a luncheon at the 101st Airborne restaurant when North told his friends about his back trouble. In late spring or early summer of 1982, a few months after Baxter's death, North invited Willard Collins and Jim Bill and Betty McInteer for lunch on board their boat on Old Hickory Lake. Descending the lake bank toward the boat, North could not understand what was wrong with his back. Avon, his wife, believed the old truck he drove around the farm was the cause. Collins teased him that he was afraid of reaching sixty.

North decided to go to specialists. They found nothing wrong with his back. They decided to do a body scan. The doctors discovered cancer. Avon, of course, was with him. The first person to see North after the doctor's visit was Willard Collins. North needed his friend. He was available.

Cancer quickly took its toll on Ira North. Baxter's death and now North's illness weighed heavily on Collins. During 1983, he called Jim Mankin, North's associate at Madison. Making conversation, Mankin asked Collins how he felt. He received an unexpected response: "How do you think I feel? Batsell's dead. Ira's dying." Following North's death in January of 1984, Collins told Ruth Byers: "My closest friends are leaving."

With North's death, Collins' four friends were dead. He no longer could turn to Jim Byers, B. C. Goodpasture, Batsell Baxter, and Ira North for advice and companionship. Indeed, a loneliness gripped Collins that could not be alleviated.

* * *

Old friendships renewed are good friendships. Franklin Camp and Willard Collins were friends and roommates in college, but each followed different directions after the Lipscomb years. Camp returned to Alabama where he gave his life to preaching. When he returned for the Lipscomb lectures in 1941, he spoke at the Thursday evening worship at Old Hickory, but little contact existed between the two men until the 1960s.

When Camp was preaching in East Gadsden, Alabama, during the early 1960s, Collins approached him about the possibility of joining the Lipscomb faculty to help train young preachers, but Camp's limited formal education would not allow him to do so. Willard Collins, however, wanted to take advantage of the expertise gained by Camp's multiplied hours of private study. He received an invitation to appear each year on the Lipscomb lectures. He has done so every year except 1980, when he had open heart surgery.

With this renewed friendship, Collins and Camp began spending much more time together. This was especially true when Camp moved to Birmingham, where he lived for twenty-three years.

"I don't have a better friend than Willard Collins," responded Franklin Camp recently. This friendship has grown since 1977 when Collins assumed the presidency of Lipscomb. On numerous occasions Collins has asked his friend to provide notes for a speech. At other times the telephone was used to get Camp's thoughts on a subject or his reaction to an idea. Camp refers to himself as an "unofficial advisor to the president."

Collins admires Camp's ability to study six and seven hours each day. Conversely, Camp admires Collins as a communicator. In fact, Camp recognizes Collins as an eloquent speaker, one who speaks with force. His ability to project his personality into his speaking is one of Collins' greatest strengths. This same personality has made Willard Collins into one of the best public relations persons Camp has seen.

The keys to Collins' success have been his balance—the ability to remain in the middle-of-the-road without losing his convictions—and his genuineness. Because of these characteristics, Camp believes Collins was the right man at the right time for the presidency of Lipscomb. In fact, Camp added: "No other person could have saved the school." Within the framework of Collins' work at Lipscomb "he has had an unusual influence on the world of young people."

With his other close friends and advisors gone, Collins has leaned rather heavily on Franklin Camp in recent years. A friend of youth became a friend again when the responsibilities of directing the fortunes of David Lipscomb College became Willard Collins' in 1977.

* * *

What are the qualities of friendship? They are best summed up in the person of Willard Collins. He is a friend to all. However, in Jim Byers, B. C. Goodpasture, Batsell Barrett Baxter, Ira North, and Franklin Camp, he has had those friends who have remained "closer than brothers."

Chapter Ten

For Such a Time as This: The Presidential Years

The previous year, beginning during the fall of 1976, had not been the best of times for Willard Collins. Something was wrong at Lipscomb. He did not quite know the source of the problems, but too many criticisms and complaints were being heard on and off campus. They could not be ignored. Faculty morale was low. Salaries for teachers from kindergarten through college were continuing to fall behind those of other schools among churches of Christ. Dissatisfaction was evident among all the school's publics. Concern was evident in the monetary support from alumni and friends.

Lipscomb's vice president had been loyal to Athens Clay Pullias almost to a fault. Yet he—along with other administrators of the school—had even thought of the drastic move of resigning in 1976. The problems facing the school had been clear for two or three years. President Pullias had painted a bleak picture for private, higher education in general and for Lipscomb in particular. Something had to be done.

Not until 1977 was the condition of the school fully known. Officially the school had balanced its budget for twenty-five consecutive years, but the Lipscomb Foundation, source for the operating funds for the school, was in debt to First American National Bank in Nashville for 3.15 million dollars. An endowment was almost non-existent. Fund raising was at a low point.

The summer of 1977 was a difficult three months on the

Lipscomb campus. The faculty and students knew something was amiss. Rumors were rampant. Thomas McMeen, vice-chairman of the Board of Directors, apprised of the school's financial condition, encouraged the board to look more deeply into the school's stability. With pressure from the Board of Directors, Athens Clay Pullias resigned from the presidency of Lipscomb on August 3, 1977. Pullias acknowledged to the *Tennessean* on August 21 that "he was considering retirement because of 'tremendous problems' facing the college."

With the impending resignation of Pullias, Willard Collins found himself in a dilemma. What should he do? There was no guarantee that the board would choose him to fill the president's chair. After all, they did not know him as a decision maker. He had remained the second person in the administration since 1946, always deferring to President Pullias. The second possibility would be an interim Collins presidency while the board selected a permanent chief executive. Would this be satisfactory to Collins? Even if he were selected as Lipscomb's president, would he receive the support of the school's many publics, including the faculty, or would he be associated with the previous administration?

These were only a few of the questions that coursed through Collins' mind during the last days of August 1977. In the meantime, a new quarter demanded special preparation. A gospel meeting called him to Pensacola, Florida, from August 28 through 30—Sunday through Tuesday. The board had met on Saturday, August 27. Pullias would resign on August 31. Collins went on to Florida, not knowing what the board might decide about his future.

On Wednesday Collins was back in Nashville. Meeting at 10:30 on the morning of September 1, the board sent for Collins. They unanimously offered him the position as president of David Lipscomb College.

The years served as Lipscomb's vice president were now behind him. New opportunities and challenges loomed ahead. For the first time Collins realized that he could no longer walk down the hall to the president's ·office, sure of finding answers to his questions. That office was now his. As Mordecai said to Esther when only she could save her people: "[A]nd who knoweth whether thou art come to the kingdom for such a time as this?" Was the new President Collins raised up ". . .for such a time as this?"

156

* * *

The Lipscomb faculty thought so. As the rumors swirled around the campus during the summer of 1977, the only name heard to fill the presidency was Willard Collins. However, Collins was not sure how the faculty would react. He even feared that many might leave Lipscomb. He had to wait until September 16 for the fall faculty meeting to discover the true feelings of his faculty. When introduced as Lipscomb's new president, he received a standing ovation.

In his formal speech to the faculty, Collins gave direction to his administration. In typical Collins fashion, he presented four areas of special concern: first, involvement—he wanted to involve literally thousands of hands in Lipscomb's future, including support organizations for all Lipscomb's schools and such special groups like Bison Boosters, an organization to support college athletics; second, direction—he wanted to make sure that Lipscomb remained close to the Lord and to the church; third, hard work—he committed himself to working hard for the school, to raise the funds necessary for the ongoing of Lipscomb; and fourth, delegation of responsibility—he did not want an administration that centered in the president's office.

In 1978 he announced his desire for four vice presidents: academics, campus affairs, business, and institutional planning. For these positions he chose Earl Dennis, Dean and Vice President for Academic Affairs; Carl McKelvey, Vice President for Campus Affairs; Edsel Holman (and then Steve Flatt), Vice President for Business Affairs; and Mack Craig, Vice President for Institutional Planning.

How would the students respond? On September 21, 1977, when the students gathered for chapel, Willard Collins, the new president, first realized that he was the "student's president." They gave him a standing ovation. Typically, Collins complimented the students. From that first chapel forward, Lipscomb's students responded favorably to their president.

Collins has always been uniquely Lipscomb. Of all the administrators, Collins was the lone man who exemplified to faculty, students, alumni, and friends of the school what Lipscomb has attempted to accomplish. He told the Nashville *Banner*: "I am kind of a symbol of this school." From 1946 to 1977 he directed student life, the recruitment of students, athletics, chapel, lectureships, and publications. Even though when he became president he relinquishedthe various responsibilities of the vice presidency, Willard Collins continued his interest in student activities. He wanted to be better accepted by the faculty. One of the first things he did was to relinquish the president's private parking place. To this day, he scrambles for an open faculty slot, just like any junior faculty member.

* * *

Responsibilities inherent to the college president's office weighed heavily on the shoulders of Willard Collins. He changed worlds. Heretofore he had dealt mainly with students. Now the major responsibility on him was the raising of immense amounts of money to sustain a campus of 3,500 students. During the first six weeks he lost ten pounds. He could not sleep. Always the question: "Who will raise the money?" His grandchildren saw a change in their grandfather. A fun man became too serious. Ruth noticed a change—impatience, nervousness.

By October the new president had become discouraged. A man of action, Collins found that things were not moving as fast as he would have liked. The reorganization of his administration was on hold while a search committee looked for a new dean. Finally Earl Dennis, who had directed the Southern Association self-study, accepted the position after having earlier removed himself from the candidates' list. This allowed the other administrators to begin their work, especially Mack Craig. His major task was to direct the campaign to raise the necessary funds to insure the school's ongoing.

Money was not as readily available to fund the school as President Collins would have liked. A campus-wide austerity program was initiated. A campaign to raise $100,000 for day-to-day operations was quickly launched. In the midst of the discouraging days of October and November, Collins opened his heart to the Executive Committee (a group of administrators and faculty representatives). Said the president: "I may have made the mistake of my life by accepting the presidency of Lipscomb." His Marshall County friend and principal of the Lipscomb elementary school, Margaret Leonard Hopper, answered his doubt: "NO! You haven't!"

By December things were much better. Collins was more comfortable in his new office. Lipscomb's supporters heard his plea for financial help; December was an excellent fund-raising month. Even though tremendous problems, mostly financial, still faced the school, Collins realized that overwhelming support was with him.

His greatest need now would be to give leadership to the great swelling tide of supporters.

GOALS FOR SUCCESS

April 13, 1979, saw the dedication of the new high school gymnasium. A large, appreciative crowd gathered as various persons were introduced who had contributed to the first new building constructed on the Lipscomb campus in ten years. Willard Collins shot the first basketball toward the goal. Cliett Goodpasture, then the Director of Development and the person responsible for raising the $715,000 to pay for the building, remembers that President Collins even asked him the location of the goal. Given the proper directions, Collins proceeded to make the first goal he tried.

The gathered friends of Lipscomb were amazed. Carl McKelvey, Vice President for Campus Affairs, suggested that some higher power must have guided that ball into the basket. Goodpasture, in awe, believed he saw the ball curve as it headed for the goal. That shot has continued to be discussed since that April night.

No one should have been overly amazed. Collins has always been adept at setting goals and then meeting them. As indicated in a previous chapter, his success as a local preacher was built on his ability to set high standards and then lead the congregations to meet attendance or contribution goals. The Old Hickory church became the largest in Davidson County during his ministry using these methods. Charlotte Avenue had to enlarge its building because Willard Collins established goals that were met.

From the first years of the Pullias-Collins administration, goals were established, slogans created. A hallmark of Lipscomb in the early years of building a senior college was "when the last brick is laid, the last dollar is paid."

Shortly after becoming president, Collins announced 1977-1978 would be The Year of Renewal. Having gone through several pessimistic years when morale was low across the campus and support waned, the call to renewal met acceptance by everyone on and off the campus. Truly, it was as if a new breeze had swept across South Nashville. Hope was recaptured; optimism again reigned.

Early in 1978, a committee of twelve, selected from the board of directors, alumni, administration, faculty, and student body, was organized to plan for Three Decisive Years encompassing 1978, 1979, and 1980. This committee became an initial planning body for David Lipscomb College. Not only were they concerned with the three years, they were challenged to develop plans for the Golden Decade, 1981-1991. At the end of the period, Lipscomb would reach its hundreth anniversary.

Important to the new goals and the slogans that evolved was a greater emphasis on long-range planning. By the fall of 1980 the committee had developed a comprehensive plan for advancement during the Golden Decade. In all, it would demand the raising of forty million dollars for new construction and endowment. Long range goals were set for the school. Indeed, it was a time to dream of what Lipscomb might become.

Specifically, Collins gave to 1978 the name "The Year of Appreciation." The previous school year had been difficult. Funds were not available for immediate faculty salary increases. Austerity was practiced across the campus. However, in 1978 the administration announced a $1,000 across-the-board raise for the teachers. As Collins has often done, he praised the faculty for their dedication and committment to Lipscomb. In all, $900,000 was allocated for faculty salary increases during the Three Decisive Years.

Lipscomb's greatest need continued to be large sums of money to retire the debt at First American National Bank. Therefore, 1980 became the Extra Million Dollar Year. At a time when interest rates reached an all time high, Lipscomb was paying one-half percent above the prime rate. During the year, the school paid $400,000 in interest alone. Before announcing the campaign to the general public, the board of directors pledged $314,500. Comedian Jerry Clower appeared at a $500 per couple dinner program, where $150,000 was raised. By June, $500,000 of the total was in hand. In January of 1981, the campaign was proclaimed a success.

The January issue of the *Lipscomb News* announced that the Three Decisive Years campaign had been a total success:

1. The bank indebtedness was significantly reduced.

2. Faculty salaries were increased by $900,000.

3. The high school gymnasium was completed without an outstanding debt.

4. Programs and services, including the Anderson Preaching Training Center, were initiated.

5. The Board of Directors increased in size.

6. The campus began a renovation, including the beautification of Bison Square.

7. Friends of Lipscomb contributed seven million dollars

to the school.
    8. Plans were formulated for the Golden Decade.

Now the Golden Decade became the emphasis. Unveiling the plans, Collins stated: "Lipscomb cannot grow without dreams and plans....[W]e want to make 'a decade of growth...a century of truth.'" Emphasizing the theme, "Crowning the First Century of Christian Education at Lipscomb," Meredith Shepherd of Washington Industries remarked: "Lipscomb has the best product in Nashville-even better than Dee Cee jeans [a product of Washington Industries]. It's up to us to sell it."

In 1984 Collins announced two goals with slogans for each. At the September faculty meeting, he urged that the following four quarters be the Year For Improving Academics. Typically Collins, the president stated: "We have squeezed you [faculty] in the past, and you have helped us with the Extra Million Dollar Year and many other special efforts. I appreciate the way you have responded. You have helped save the school from a crisis." On October 7 the Development Council met. A major capital campaign was announced as a part of the Golden Decade. Called "When the Centuries Meet," plans were announced to raise $35 million by 1991 when the school would begin its second century.

It may have been an accident, but the amazing goal made by President Collins at the opening of the high school gymnasium was an omen for his entire administration. With high expectations and slogans to express those goals, the Collins administration has been a decided success.

THE STUDENTS' PRESIDENT

"I am pleased to be known as the Students' president."—Willard Collins, Bison Day, November 1, 1985.

It was not quite the typical Bison Day, the official opening of the basketball season at Lipscomb, like others that Willard Collins had participated in as both president and vice president. The social clubs weres limited to signs hanging about McQuiddy Gymnasium. However, this did not stop the student body from showing their appreciation for their president. When Collins began reading the proclamation declaring the day Bison Day, the students could not restrain themselves. They were already standing. Quickly one student, then another, then several, finally twenty or thirty mobbed Collins with mementoes of Bison Day. Only their president could have as much fun with them in such a manner.

Other Bison Days ran quickly through his mind. This one on November 1, 1985 would be his last, but the memories of previous ones would remain vivid for a lifetime. On numerous occasions he had been carried on the shoulders of students around the gym bedecked in the wildest kinds of dress. On one occasion—wearing an aviator's helmet and goggles—he even rode a hot air balloon a few feet off the ground. These were the kinds of thing that have made him the Students' President.

When Collins accepted the presidency he was not willing to quit his role as presider over chapel. Vice President Carl McKelvey was in charge, but Collins continued his long-time role during one chapel each day—except those days when the school's business took him from the campus. His optimism was readily appreciated by the students. They could feel his concern for them. They could laugh with and at him. In fact, on numerous occasions he would encourage laughter and fun by his own designed—or sometimes undesigned—remarks. Whether the sun was shining, or the temperature was 0, or rain was pelting down, or snow made movement hazardous, his "Enjoy the weather" statements were always enjoyed. Each day chapel ended with his familiar "That is all."

Beginning with the June graduation of 1977, the seniors showed their appreciation of both Lipscomb and Collins in unique ways. Collins' first June graduation brought quite a surprise. As the graduates accepted their diplomas, they shook the president's hand. Coins began to fall to the floor. Collins could not understand what was happening: "I thought I had a hole in my pocket. I didn't know where the money was coming from at first. The more money that came, the faster Dean Craig called the names. I wanted to tell him to slow down, money was coming so fast." They gave something over five dollars in small coins, but it was a gesture appreciated by their president. Since that first surprise, the graduates have given larger amounts to show their love for Willard Collins.

On June 2, 1979, the graduating class proclaimed their day "Willard Collins' Day." In a proclamation they stated: "We are proud to call him our president." The proclamation then cited his "outstanding qualities of leadership, guidance and wisdom" and his "instilling in us the importance of being the truly spirited men and women that we are capable of being." The graduates noted especially his involvement in campus life.

President Collins encouraged a change in student government

on campus. But the only input he had was giving a name to the organization—the All Students' Association. The name was a revival of the one used for the student government he helped organize when he was a student at Lipscomb. In fact, he was the first president of ASA.

David Sampson, student body president, led in the writing of a constitution for the All Students' Association. Numerous students from across the campus participated. When finished the student body readily accepted the document. It called for more representation than any previous student government with senators from each class and several at-large representatives. Again, Willard Collins had showed himself as the Students' President.

The most ambitious project ever undertaken by students at Lipscomb was the beautification of Bison Square—the area between the Dining Center and Alumni Auditorium. Under the leadership of Paul Nance, president of ASA, and Karen Horn, secretary, the student body contributed $6,000 during the last week of classes in the spring quarter of 1979. Solicitation of funds and material continued through the school year of 1979-1980. By the fall of 1980, the square needed only minor touching up. In all, the students raised $50,000 in cash and materials donated. Accomplishment came because of the atmosphere evident on campus. The impact of President Collins was the key to success.

Birthdays have been popular times to honor Collins. Among the most memorable occasions was November 1979. In an event planned by Chris Smith, the president of the student body surprised Collins with a cake in the Bison Room. Following the festivities, the students went with the Collinses to Alumni Auditorium where they viewed one of President Collins' favorite films, "Follow Me Boys". Collins knew from this gesture that the students supported him. He was their president.

Not to be outdone by Chris Smith, the 1985-86 ASA not only had a party for Collins, they also sold Willard Collins' shirts and "I love Willard" buttons. The shirts had Collins' likeness on the front. On the back was the statement "Forty-two years of service" with "That is all" beneath it. The students bought both the shirt and the button by the hundreds and wore them on campus. On November 12, when the president reached his seventieth birthday, a campus-wide party, led by ASA president Tim Gobble and secretary Ginger Johnson, was enjoyed by all, especially by Willard Collins.

The Collins' home has been open to Lipscomb students from his first years of presidency. Especially enjoyable for all has been the standing invitation for faculty and students to share July 4 with them at their home. The faculty furnished home-made ice cream and cookies for all summer quarter students. Following the ice cream, everyone sat in a circle, singing their favorite hymns. In 1985 he declined Opryland owner Edward Gaylord's invitation to lead the dedicatory prayer on the gala opening voyage of the *General Jackson* Showboat because he and Ruth had already invited the students to their home.

When the formal freshman reception was dropped, the Collinses substituted a party at their home. Again the faculty furnished the ice cream and cookies. In extending the invitation to the freshmen, Collins on one occasion stated: "The faculty will furnish the ice cream and cookies. Ruth and I will furnish the grass." Not knowing the street talk for marijuana, he did not understand until later that the students had another laugh at his expense. Typically, he told the story often during the last years of his presidency.

The ice cream social and other unselfish acts, along with his readiness to enjoy life with the students, are among the reasons Willard Collins will be remembered as the Students' President.

On January 7, 1986, a special chapel was held to celebrate the "Million Dollar Day" in honor of Willard Collins. Central to the events was a framed statement to Collins from the students represented by ASA president Tim Gobble and secretary Ginger Johnson. The resolution read:

> As long as there is a David Lipscomb College, students will hold the name of Willard Collins in high esteem. Those who were fortunate enough to have been students during Brother Collins' tenure will always remember his caring attitude, and the loving, fatherly hand he was ever ready to lend. They will remember how he always seemed to make chapel a fresh, rewarding experience. They will remember how he taught them, by his own example, to find something good in every situation. Every time they think of David Lipscomb, they'll think of him.
>
> No one could ever replace Brother Collins. No individual could ever fill his shoes. But the imprint he made, the legacy of love he left, will always endure.
>
> And "That is all."
> The Students of David Lipscomb College

> January 7, 1986
> /s/ Tim Gobble /s/ Ginger Johnson
> President/Secretary

* * *

A FAMILY AFFAIR

Bob Neil says Willard Collins "retained the common touch" bred into him by his Marshall County upbringing. Undoubtedly this characteristic has endeared him to everyone with whom he has come into contact during his preaching, his involvement at Lipscomb, and his contacts with the business community. This "common touch" is mentioned by all who talk about Willard and Ruth Collins.

David Lipscomb College during its junior college days was a close-knit family. It was certainly true when the Collinses were students. But, according to Collins and his brother-in-law Bud Morris, the school lost that close, family atmosphere when it became a senior college with many more students. Both remember the days when E. H. Ijams was president and the school song was S. P. Pittman's "Busy and Happy at DLC."

It was Ruth Collins who announced that she and her husband wanted the Lipscomb community to be like a family affair. The president has done his part to develop the family atmosphere, but the person most responsible has been Ruth Collins.

In an interview with David England, the director of the Lipscomb News Bureau, Mrs. Collins stated:

> Willard and I have always felt, and still do, that the president needs to be with the people, not elevated in any way, bringing love, companionship and everything to make people feel close and free with us. We decided that one way we could do it, since I enjoy cooking, was to have a good many of the things on the campus here in these [president's] quarters.

She accomplished her goals by preparing meals for many of the Lipscomb support groups and for special guests on the campus.

Business men from the community were often amazed that Mrs. Collins prepared and served the meals. Letters were received from officers of First American National Bank complimenting the home-like touch given to their visits by Lipscomb's First Lady.

The attitude Mrs. Collins had toward members of the board and businessmen paralleled the feelings she had toward the entire campus family. Continuing her interview, she remarked:

That was exactly the theme we talked about before he ever took [the presidency], that we were going to bring a close, Christian, family feeling to the campus from the elementary school right on through all of them [high school and college]. We still try to do that. We are fully aware of the good job they are doing and we want them to feel close to us, but not feel that we are someone elevated to a pedestal in any way. We're right here working with them and we appreciate what they're doing.

Furthermore, the attitude she possessed as the president's wife made a difference: "I don't feel myself one bit above any of the others—administrator's wives, people on this campus—I don't want to. I don't want them to look up to me....It's my nature. And Willard is a very humble man."

The Collinses' "common touch" extended to the faculty throughout their tenure at Lipscomb. His concern as to the acceptance by the faculty in 1977 was totally unfounded. He had always been the major link of the faculty to the administration. His office was always open to any member of the faculty who wanted to talk.

This same concern was carried down the hall to the president's office. It was an open office, but many reluctantly entered for fear of disturbing the new executive. Under the Collins administration, many of the faculty benefits were restored, including faculty discounts for children in all the schools. The board changed the kinship rule for employment at Lipscomb to exclude only the kin of board members, the president, and vice presidents. Husbands and wives, fathers and sons were allowed to hold faculty rank for the first time since the late 1940s.

Lipscomb's faculty, over the years, has been relatively stable. In response to the long years of service, the Collins' administration began a program of recognizing its faculty. At first, plaques with the number of years served were given. In 1983 the school began honoring all faculty and staff with twenty-five or more years of service with an engraved watch along with five-year strips for the plaques.

To encourage and recognize good teaching, the administration initiated the outstanding teacher awards in 1979. That first year the awards went to Dr. Harvey Floyd and Dr. Marlin Connelly. Each award included a check for a thousand dollars. In recent years, Dr. Alton Baker of Birmingham, Alabama, a Lipscomb graduate, endowed the John William Baker Summer Fellowship Awards worth five thousand dollars each. The first recipient was Dr. Willis Owens of the biology department in 1981.

Even though a college of 2,300 students cannot have the same family atmosphere as a school of 300, the closeness generated by the Collins years has moved the school much nearer a family affair.

* * *

A BRIDGE BUILDER

Alienation is not a word in Willard Collins' vocabulary. He wants to be friends with everybody and wants everybody to be his friend. This does not suggest that he has been totally successful in his desire. All of his decisions have not made everyone happy. His loyalties, on occasion, have caused him to have blind spots, but for someone to be angry with him or with Lipscomb has always caused Lipscomb's president deep concern.

One characteristic, therefore, of Willard Collins' administration has been the building of bridges within the school and with the school's various publics, including churches. As soon as he accepted the presidency of Lipscomb, he announced as first order of business the construction of a high school gymnasium. For many years the patrons across the campus in the elementary school and high school had been promised new facilities, including a new elementary school and a gymnasium. Campaigns were held to raise money for the facilities, but nothing was forthcoming. Therefore, Collins moved quickly to build bridges to a rather large support group centered in the area of Lipscomb's greatest support, Nashville.

Cliett Goodpasture accepted the responsibility to oversee the raising of the funds. On faith, ground was broken in May 1978. Clarence Shaub, long-time Lipscomb supporter, served as general contractor. Even though the funds were not contributed as quickly as Collins would have liked, the gym was opened on April 13, 1979 with great fanfare. The width of the gulf narrowed between the administration and parents on the Granny White Pike side of the campus.

A second step to close the chasm came when plans for the Reese L. Smith, Jr. Athletic Complex were unveiled on February 7, 1980. An ambitious project, it would provide the high school with a complete athletic facility including a football stadium, baseball field, track, and parking facilities. The cost estimate exceeded the school's ability to pay. Into the breach stepped Nile Yearwood, the contractor who had constructed many of the buildings on campus at an earlier date. With his contacts, Yearwood was able to construct the complex at half the estimated cost.

A third project long promised to Lipscomb's patrons was an elementary school building. In the early 1960s the school solicited funds toward that goal, but nothing was forthcoming. This alienated many supporters of Lipscomb. Collins renewed the project. The Golden Decade program designated over two million dollars for the building. In 1985 a twenty-five year dream came to fruition when the Metropolitan government declared Burton School surplus property. In an open bid, Lipscomb secured the building and eight acres of land for $752,000. With the spending of $1,500,000 to refurbish and expand the existing facilities, the elementary school was to have a new home in August 1986.

Willard Collins felt a strong need to reach out to the alumni of Lipscomb. Over the years a number of things had happened that had alienated large segments of former students. The 1943 rupture that saw E. H. Ijams step down as president of the school was of major proportions. The issue of premillennialism was the wedge that divided the faculty and the supporters of Lipscomb. Little attempt at healing the wound was made until the presidency of Willard Collins.

In 1935 the senior class, sponsored by Charles Brewer, constructed the campus bell tower on the lawn in front of Harding Hall. Following the division of 1943, the tower was never referred to as Brewer Tower. Early in the first year of Collins' administration, he made a decision to call it Brewer Tower. During Homecoming 1978 the family gathered at the tower to see an unveiling of a plaque commemorating Charles Brewer's contributions to the school he had helped Willard Collins grow to love.

The school completed the bridging of a major chasm in 1985 when the lecture auditorium adjacent to McFarland Science Hall was named for Dr. J. S. Ward, the father of Robbie Brewer, the wife of Charles. Other Ward descendants included Truman Ward, for a long time associated with WLAC radio in Nashville and a very successful businessman. He was a member of Lipscomb's Board of Directors prior to the rupture of 1943 when four members of the nine-member board resigned.

During the last years of the Pullias administration, Robert Neil, who had lost his job at Lipscomb as a result of the 1943 division, returned to the campus on two occasions to organize reunions. One reunion was of the singers he had directed in past years; the other was for baseball players whom he had coached. These endeavors were so successful that Bob Neil became a frequent visitor on the campus early in Collins' presidency.

Neil was a graduate of Lipscomb, class of 1929. Fifty years later he organized a reunion of the class. As a result of that meeting, the Golden Circle began. The only requirement was having attended Lipscomb fifty years earlier. On August 8, 1980 the first official Golden Circle group met on campus. It was the beginning of a very important bridge with Lipscomb's past. President Collins remarked to the first meeting: "In 25 years we will overflow this building. . . .We anticipate it [the Golden Circle] becoming one of the most important dates on the Lipscomb calendar." Collins was correct. Each year sees a larger group gathered than the year previous.

E. H. Ijams' nine-year tenure as president ended in 1943. His involvement with Lipscomb reached back to 1922 when he spent four years on the faculty before becoming the minister for the Central Church of Christ in Nashville. Many students passed through Harding Hall during his association with the school. However, he had little contact with Lipscomb from 1943 until Willard Collins became president in 1977.

A number of his friends, including Paul Brown and Bob Neil, encouraged Collins to honor the former president in the same manner. Collins quickly agreed. He had attended Lipscomb under Ijams's presidency and was fond of the former president. Plans were made to bring Ijams from Memphis to Nashville on November 8, 1979. It was an important occasion for Lipscomb. Many who had been alienated from the school were present to honor their friend. Announced at the occasion was the Ijams Professorship of Religious Education to be funded by his friends. The plans were to raise $150,000 in Memphis and Nashville. In 1982 Dr. John Harris, a Lipscomb graduate who had taught in a number of universities across the South, was the first Ijams Professor of Religious Education. The bridge building continued.

In another effort to bridge the gap between the school and its alumni, the College established an "Alumnus of the Year" award in 1980. At the Alumni Association Dinner on April 26, Ira North received the first award. Governor Lamar Alexander, the speaker for the occasion, remarked: "It [the selection of Ira North as Alumnus of the Year] signifies, I suspect, the legacy of David Lipscomb.

It says something about the values and goals of the teachings and the attitudes and the academics here [at Lipscomb]."

A complaint, whether true or false, Collins often heard was the distance separating churches of Christ and David Lipscomb College. To remedy the deficit, the school's administration moved quickly to enlarge its visibility in the training of young men and women to enter foreign missions. In 1978 the missionary-in-residence program began. The Vultee church in Nashville established a chair in missions. In the same year funds were forthcoming from the will of Dan Gray, long-time elder for the church in Old Hickory and father of Dr. Joe Gray of the Lipscomb faculty, to establish the Dan Gray Missionary Center on the Lipscomb campus. Two years later the first World Mission Forum convened at Lipscomb.

Also in 1978 the old Cockrell House was renovated to become the Anderson Preacher Training Center in honor of J. C. Anderson, the second president of the Nashville Bible School. Dr. Tom Holland became head of the program. At the same time the Nashville School of Preaching moved from the Hillsboro church building to the Anderson Center. Under the direction of Holland, the school continued throughout the presidency of Collins, but under the name of the Nashville Bible School. It was restructured as an evening program for men and women who did not wish to attend college for credit but wished to continue their learning toward becoming better workers in the church.

By building bridges early in his administration, Collins was able to rally thousands of people to the cause of Christian education at Lipscomb. The increased enrollment, the growing resources of the school, and the new construction reflected the confidence emerging from the many publics of David Lipscomb College.

* * *

NINE YEARS OF GROWTH

Willard Collins' successes prior to becoming president of Lipscomb should have made it easy to predict that he would be a builder. While he was at both Old Hickory and Charlotte Avenue, the churches engaged in rather large building programs. Such construction went naturally with Collins' penchant for goal setting.

Two things were necessary for Lipscomb to renew her growth that had slowed over the previous several years. First, student recruitment had to be enlarged. In part, the bridge building with the churches had a positive impact on attracting new students. Even though the faculty changed but little, parents seemed somewhat more trusting with Collins at the helm. Second, funds were necessary in larger amounts to accomplish the goals outlined in the Three Decisive Years and the Golden Decade campaigns. The total price tag for both campaigns would exceed forty million dollars. This figure does not include the ever-increasing budgets of the school that reached $16.7 million for 1985-86.

Collins' first year, 1977-78, was a year for planning. Not until 1978 did fundraising show a marked increase. In 1977 the school had a Thanksgiving campaign that raised $184,000. Again at Thanksgiving in 1978, a campaign that raised $150,000 honored Batsell Barrett Baxter. Collins could relax somewhat after January 1979 because the contributions to the school were mounting in record dollars. From September 1, 1978 to January 31, 1979, a total of $1 million was contributed to the school. To show the increases in support, the following numbers are interesting:

1975-76	$815,000
1976-77	1,175,000
1977-78	1,700,000
1978-79	2,000,000

Alumni giving increased from $290,000 in 1976-77 to $560,000 in 1978-79.

In March 1979, President Collins responded to the increased generosity of Lipscomb supporters:

It is wonderful how the stream is flowing! We must all keep our efforts and do all we can this year to build Lipscomb. . . .I want to send my personal thanks for what so many of you have done during the time I have been in my new role. Lipscomb is our school, and the future is unlimited if we stay close to the Lord and really work together.

A major thrust of the 1978-79 fundraising campaign emphasized the construction of the high school gymnasium. Two other major concerns included the liquidation of the debt and increased teacher salaries. All the while, small amounts were added to the endowment. The Extra Million Dollar Year in 1980 was ticketed entirely for debt reduction. The special drive pushed the total giving for

1979-80 over $3,000,000 for the first time in the school's history.

For three consecutive years, beginning in 1979, the school established record enrollments, reaching the highest figure in 1981 with 2,375 students. An enlarged student body made new facilities increasingly important. Now the administration turned to the college side of the campus to construct a new residence hall for women, following the same formula used for constructing the Reese Smith Athletic Complex. Nile Yearwood volunteered his services, thereby cutting in half the construction costs of the building. The cost estimate of the building was $565,000. The final cost was $528,000 or twenty-one dollars per square foot. With the dedication of the new hall, the name Yearwood was placed over the entrance. It was an honor well deserved.

Some years are bigger than others. They are more easily remembered. For Willard Collins, one such year was 1982. Yearwood Hall began construction in January. In February, at the board meeting, the payment of the $3.15 million debt was celebrated by burning the note. This had been virtually Priority One from Day One of Collins' administration. This debt had drained the school in interest of $2,838,880 over a twenty-year period.

For several years, the business faculty, headed by Axel Swang, had been urging the school to construct adequate facilities for business administration. The debt had to be retired before any campaign could be undertaken. A major push for the construction came from Dr. Harold Sutton of Bradenton, Florida and Fred Sutton of Melbourne, Florida. Dr. Sutton had attended Lipscomb for a short while before going elsewhere to concentrate on medicine. Fred Sutton had graduated from Lipscomb with a business major. The brothers wanted to do something for Lipscomb and at the same time honor Dr. Axel Swang, long-time chairman of the business administration department. Therefore, they committed $350,000 toward the construction of the Swang Center for Business Administration. A stipulation for the gift by the brothers was that Swang's name must appear on the structure. Other gifts were contributed, including a matching grant of $200,000 from the Kresge Foundation. The building opened for classes during the fall of 1984. The total cost exceeded two million dollars.

Lipscomb became involved in computers several years previously, but most services were leased either from Vanderbilt University or companies in the city. In September 1982, a Digital Equipment Corporation VAX 11/780 computer was installed at a cost of over

$500,000. Lipscomb, in a big way, entered the computer age during Collins' administration. Since that time, almost every department has added computer capabilities.

With a total of $3,849,159.49 invested in construction from 1977-1984, it was time to move in other directions. Already in 1983, a National Development Board was organized to raise thirty million dollars for endowment. The school owned a major piece of property that held the key to reaching the goal before 1991, the school's centennial. A. M. Burton had long been the largest benefactor of Lipscomb. Besides his monetary gifts, he left his home and acreage, Seven Hills, to Lipscomb at his death. In 1982 the school began planning for the development of the 190 acres. In the face of neighborhood opposition, the plans were withdrawn.

Instead of the school developing Seven Hills, a decision was made to invite large development companies to submit plans and bids for the property. After sifting through numerous proposals, Jerry Carroll and his associates were selected. A Nashville developer, his company was able to accomplish what Lipscomb could not. Even though opposition remained strong, the Lipscomb community rallied to the cause at neighborhood meetings and through letters to Tandy Wilson, the councilman for the district.

Carroll orchestrated his plans well. His development was not as commercially-oriented as previous plans. The highest hills were not developed. When the plans were refined, the Davidson County Planning Commission unanimously accepted the development on March 14, 1984. At that point councilman Wilson asked the entire council to accept the proposal. They did so on May 14, 1984. On June 28, 1984 the school received a check for $11,250,000 from Jerry Carroll.

With endowment already invested, the school was half way to the announced goal of $30,000,000 for endowment. At the end of 1985, the total funds invested amounted to $19,500,000. The sum represents a huge growth since September 1977 when the endowment was almost non-existent. Endowment income amounted to $145,397 in August 1977. By August 31, 1985, the income was $1,424,243.

Besides large sums of money needed to operate a campus of 3,600 students and more physical facilities needed to house these students, the school began to explore new academic programs. At the undergraduate level, a major in social work was added. To develop the program, Jean Bowman, former Deputy Commissioner of

Human Services for Tennessee, joined the faculty. With the purchase of the VAX computer, new majors emphasizing the latest computer technology were offered. Under the leadership of Dr. Ralph Butler, Lipscomb developed an outstanding computer program

As a part of the Golden Decade, a proposal for a graduate program in Bible was announced in 1981. Carl McKelvey, Vice President for Campus Affairs, accepted the chairmanship of the Bible Advisory Committee. Already the Board of Directors had approved the concept. For two years the planning committee functioned until March 10, 1983 when the Masters Degree in Bible was announced at a special dinner. Dr. William Woodson, formerly chairman of the Bible department at Freed-Hardeman College, became the coordinator of the initial graduate program at Lipscomb. The first students enrolled for classes in the fall of 1983. At the June graduation in 1985, Allen Burris became the first M. A. graduate of David Lipscomb College.

By any standard of measurement, Willard Collins' years as president of David Lipscomb College were ones of growth. The new buildings, the retirement of the huge debt, the increased giving by Lipscomb's friends, the sale of the Burton property, the establishment of the school's first major endowment, and the purchase of the Burton School property indicate a very successful nine years in the president's office.

THE CHANGE OF LEADERSHIP

Willard Collins would reach the mandatory retirement age of seventy in November 1985. It was time to begin the search for a new president. In the minds of many people, Collins was irreplaceable. But in January 1985, the Board of Directors appointed a search committee with W. B. Bennett, Vice Chairman of the board as chairman. The committee included 10 board members, along with Willard Collins and a faculty representative, Dr. Robert Kerce.

After in-depth studies as to what qualities the next president of Lipscomb should possess, a nation-wide search began for the right person. Chairman Bennett traveled at his own expense to interview candidates and to get input from knowledgeable persons across the breadth of the United States. Anticipation was high on the campus. Who would be the next president? Names were suggested to the faculty representative. Should the new president come from on campus or should the committee recommend an off-campus person? The consensus of the faculty emerged in favor of an off-campus person.

On Wednesday, October 23, 1985, the selection committee met to make its selection for proposal to the full Board of Directors, scheduled to meet on Saturday, October 26. A first decision was not forthcoming until a special 7:30 A.M. meeting on the day of the board meeting. The committee unanimously recommended Dr. Harold Hazelip, Dean of the Harding Graduate School of Religion, minister of the Highland Avenue church in Memphis, and speaker on the national *Herald of Truth* television program, as its candidate for the next president of David Lipscomb. The board, meeting in its regular fall session, unanimously accepted the selection committee's recommendation. Lipscomb had a new president-elect.

Lipscomb's faculty gathered at the annual Faculty-Staff dinner that evening with greater anticipation than exhibited in recent years. The dinner finished, the long-awaited announcement was about to be made. Who would it be? Chairman of the Board of Directors, Tom McMeen, made the announcement that Dr. Hazelip would be the next president of Lipscomb. It was a welcomed selection. The faculty expressed its approval.

However, the greatest approval given that night was for the one who had led Lipscomb for the eight previous years, Willard Collins. When introduced by Tom Holland, those present stood as one. It was a loving recognition of what he had accomplished since that fateful September 1, 1977 when named president of the college.

Collins' statement about the function of David Lipscomb College made in September 1981 suggests why he was so well-liked by the faculty of Lipscomb.

> We are a happy community—we are positive for the right and against the wrong. We are seeking to help build the Christian Family as we encourage young people to meet, fall in love and marry at the proper time as they are trained at Lipscomb. We want to provide solutions for apathy in the church and to encourage an evangelistic spirit....As A. M. Burton said, "Christian education is the hope of the world."

How did Lipscomb students react to the presidential change? Interviewed by *The Babbler*, the campus newspaper, the students indicated again their affection for their president. "I think Dr. Hazelip is really a good choice [for the presidency]," said Tom Carden. "He's been involved in Christian education and the development of the church, but it's going to be hard to replace Brother Collins." Even first-quarter freshmen had developed a strong relationship toward Collins. "I'll miss President Collins," said freshman Melissa Hite. "I've only been here a short time, but I've grown to love him a lot and I'll miss him, but I'm sure Dr. Hazelip will be just as nice."

The Babbler concluded: "Many students...seemed more interested in talking about the outgoing president than the one who will replace him." Indicative of this feeling was the reaction of David Dowdy. "It'll be hard for Dr. Hazelip to be as open as Brother Collins has been. It always seemed like Brother Collins has been genuinely concerned." Probably Dwayne Barrett summed up the attitude of most students: "I think Dr. Hazelip will do a lot for the school. The committee made an excellent choice, but I'll be sorry to see Brother Collins go."

PRESIDENT COLLINS LOOKS AT HIS ADMINISTRATION

He would not know it early in his administration, but looking back over eight years as president of David Lipscomb College Collins could say that he had a much rougher time as vice president than as president. For this reason Collins could look backward during the fall of 1985 and list numerous enjoyable experiences as president. His list of disappointing experiences was minimal.

Enjoyable Experiences

1. High school gymnasium dedication and the dedication of the Reese Smith, Jr. Athletic Complex. Especially remembered was the ball going through the hoop.

2. The Word Bennett gift of $500,000.

3. The day the planning committee approved the rezoning of the Burton property.

4. The delivery of the check of $11,250,000 as payment for the Burton property.

5. The payment of the debt and the burning of the note in the president's quarters.

6. The dedication of the Swang Center and the $850,000 gifts of the Sutton brothers.

7. The purchase of the Burton school property.

8. Birthday parties given by students.

9. Standing ovation at Homecoming 1978, his first year as president.

10. The dinner in honor of Ruth Collins, November 1985. Over

$50,000 raised for scholarships.

11. The visit of former President Ford, November 4, 1985.

12. Winning the NAIA National basketball championship, March 1986.

Most Difficult Experiences

1. The first six weeks of presidency.

2. The first zoning meeting on the Burton property. Collins was heckled and a decision by the zoning commission was deferred.

* * *

Willard Collins' key to success throughout his life has been his ability to relate to people. He has truly been a people person.

In response to a question as to the characteristics he possessed that have been important to his success, he listed as his strongest characteristic his ability to meet people and his penchant for carrying on a conversation. Second, he always attempted to make life positive and happy. He believed life is worth living. Third, Collins believed he knew the value of a dollar. When he was a young man a dollar bill was as "big as a bedspread." Thus, he could appreciate any gift given to Lipscomb, whether small or large.

Looking toward the coming of Dr. Harold Hazelip as the new president of Lipscomb, what did Collins believe he was leaving as a legacy? He first mentioned an endowment of $19.5 million. Then he suggested a sound organization centered in the four vice presidents of Lipscomb. He added: "We have shown the value of involvement." He concluded by stating: "I hope the school is a little closer to the Lord."

* * *

On June 11, 1985, the *20th Century Christian* Publishing company hosted a luncheon during Lipscomb's summer Lectureship. An invited guest was President Willard Collins. Typically, he did not suspect that he was the honored guest. At the conclusion of the meal, Mark McInteer, speaking in behalf of the entire organization, named Willard Collins their Christian Leadership Award honoree. Responding to the presentation, Collins stated: "This was a total surprise to me. I appreciate this so much, and having all of you, whom I have known and loved, here. Thank you [Mark McInteer] for the message. It means more to me coming from *20th Century Christian*, people who are so close to me."

This humility was ever characteristic of Willard Collins. When asked how he personally felt about his presidency, he responded: "It is the climax of a good life. Sometimes it scares me that things have gone so well."

He was "raised up for such a time as this."

Chapter Eleven

Honor to Whom Honor
Tributes from His Friends

Willard Collins' life has touched and influenced countless individuals during his public career. This chapter includes representative samples of tributes from his friends. It includes preachers who have been a part of Collins' life since the 1930s. Since returning Lipscomb in 1943, he has been closely associated with administrators of other Christian colleges. These are represented by several presidents and former presidents of the schools. Graduates of Lipscomb are included. All of them have special memories of their friend. Two special tributes are included from the widows of his closest friends—Batsell Barrett Baxter and Ira North. From the present Lipscomb faculty a number of one-line statements are included.

Whether one line or five hundred words, all the tributes say the same thing: Willard Collins has had a major impact on the lives of thousands of people. Each tribute speaks for itself. He is worthy of honor for a life well lived before God and the world.

* * *

A most pleasing aspect of this Administration has been America's return to those Christian values upon which this nation was founded and which made it great two centuries ago. Institutions based on these principles, such as David Lipscomb College, not only emphasize these fundamentals but also take a burden off the public sector. Men such as Willard Collins who head these institutions serve one of the most noble purposes in our land today.

Willard Collins does not serve as David Lipscomb College's president because it is fashionable or noble. He does so because he believes in its foundation and because he serves the Lord. He has done so for half a century, regardless of trends or national priorities.

It is my sincere pleasure to salute and commend George Willard Collins for service to his college, his country, and his God.

Ronald Reagan
President of the United States

* * *

Willard Collins typifies so many things which make Tennessee the great state that it is. A country boy with modest background, he was blessed with parents who wanted the best for him, both from this world and from a better world to come. He set his sights high and then used his own initiative and the advantages available to all Tennesseans to reach the top of his profession.

David Lipscomb College is a marvelous asset to our state, and much of its greatness comes from the leadership that Willard Collins has provided it for nearly half a century.

Throughout President Collins' tenure, David Lipscomb College has trained Tennessee young people to be better citizens and part of our state's efficient, productive work force. Again, Willard Collins has been at the forefront of his college's success in training these citizens.

All Tennesseans join me in saluting Willard Collins for his wonderful service to his school and to his native state.

Lamar Alexander
Governor of Tennessee

* * *

Nashville owes an immeasurable debt to Willard Collins for his role in leading the training of young Christian men and women to take their place in society. It is, of course, David Lipscomb College which does the training, but overthe last forty years and more, the names Willard Collins and David Lipscomb College have become virtually synonymous.

Many of Lipscomb's students have, and continue to, come from

Nashville. And many more have been students who came here as strangers and then elected to make their homes here permanently as working, productive citizens who recognize the natural and acquired assets of Tennessee's capital city.

President Collins has led Lipscomb in major expansion during his nine-year tenure. His leadership in developing the Burton property adds quality to Nashville's life. The new buildings on the Lipscomb campus add beauty to the school and gives stature to the City of Nashville as a city of colleges.

On behalf of the citizens of Nashville, I congratulate Willard Collins on his retirement and commend him for his service to his adopted city.

Richard Fulton
Mayor of Metropolitan
Nashville/Davidson County

* * *

Nashville is fortunate to claim Willard Collins as a Christian and civil leader.

Since beginning his preaching career at Old Hickory Church of Christ, Willard has demonstrated great concern for each individual he spiritually touched. He has encouraged many, leading religious meetings and conferences throughout the South, including the full-house when Nashville's Municipal Auditorium opened in 1962.

David Lipscomb College is one of this area's leading institutions, and Willard Collins' influence has helped it become so. He is a major contributor to the heritage of the Christian College, instructing Bible classes since 1944. Anyone who asks will find that many Church of Christ elders, deacons, and preachers have been led in some way by this man.

The community is a better place to live, work, andworship because of Willard's leadership of Lipscomb. A network of leaders, spread throughout the nation, received much of their training and counseling at Lipscomb while Willard Collins was at the helm.

I am proud to claim Willard as a friend. I have enjoyed and been uplifted through our long association. He is an inspiration.

Kenneth L. Roberts, Chairman
and Chief Executive Officer
First American Corporation

* * *

Throughout history the enduring success of any group has been determined by the integrity and moral fiber of the people within that group. Corruption and dishonesty have played major roles in the decline of all the great empires of the world. Lack of integrity in business has cut short the lifespan and success of many companies. Surely the continued success of America depends on instilling high moral principles within our young people.

I have known Willard for many years, and have been more closely associated with him during the last few years. I can truly say to you that Willard Collins has spent his life combating through Christian education the things I have just mentioned. Instead, he has instilled integrity, high moral character, honesty and the highest of principles in the students at Lipscomb.

The great teachings of Christianity, emphasizing personal integrity and a genuine concern for others, I believe, hold the key to personal success and the hope for the continued progress of our western civilization. David Lipscomb College, under the guidance of Willard Collins' leadership, has been a source of teaching these principles within the Nashville community.

Willard Collins has played a key roll in the growth of David Lipscomb College for over 40 years. Under his leadership, the college has grown from a small junior college to a four year liberal arts college offering graduate studies in Bible and Business. Brother Collins has insisted that the college adhere to its principles of daily Bible study and Chapel. High academic standards have been maintained and raised consistently through the years.

I have been very impressed with the high level of admission to medical school from David Lipscomb College. In Nashville, we have a great number of outstanding physicians who are not only professionally and scientifically outstanding, but even more importantly, they are deeply concerned with the emotional and moral character of their patients, as well as the primary illnesses.

I personally strongly believe the foundation of these principles that are now put into practice had the roots established when the young men attended DLC under the direct influence of Willard Collins.

But perhaps the most significant contributions Willard Collins has made to the lives of the many young people he has trained has been showing, through example, an optimistic attitude, good humor and great love for other people from all walks of life.

This compassion and kindness is truly Willard's greatest tribute, which will endure through many, many years to come, not only at DLC, but in the Nashville community as well!

Dr. Thomas Frist, Sr.
Chief Medical Officer
Hospital Corporation of America

* * *

Years ago, the college presidents of the brotherhood, together with their vice-presidents and/or deans met in Tulsa, Oklahoma (This was before Oklahoma Christian's move to its present campus). Willard Collins was arranging for the college presidents to ride together in a bus to a certain point in the city, and as the bus took off, one of the presidents remarked, "My! What I would give to have a vice-president like Willard Collins!" This was and is Willard Collins—energetic, cheerful, and keenly conscious of the welfare of others.

Nature was kind to Willard Collins—tall, handsome, and a million dollar voice. If he had used that voice in the entertainment or political world instead of to the glory of God, he would now be financially able upon his retirement to see the world.

As Vice President and later as President of David Lipscomb College, Collins pressed for high academic standards, but at no time did he put standards above high spiritual ideals characteristic of Bible instruction.

Willard Collins is, spiritually speaking, a full-grown Christian: ethical and honest; sincere and dedicated; kind and sympathetic; humble and consecrated; energetic and enthusiastic. He has served well his Master, his brethren, and the members of his own family. To God be the glory!

Rex A. Turner, President
Alabama Christian School
of Religion

* * *

The early 1950's were my teenage years. Charlotte Avenue Church of Christ was our family's church home and Willard Collins was our minister.

During those formative years he exerted a very powerful influence for good in my life. To remember those years is to recall how many lives in that community he influenced.

His sermons were evangelistic and called for overt response. The church grew numerically and spiritually. While his preaching was powerful it does not explain his total effectiveness. He was typically interested in people and quietly involved in their lives.

He was an innovative local minister. He stressed the importance of Bible school as the key to church growth and insisted on an active program of Christian education. He initiated a weekly church bulletin as a news source for the congregation.

His work with and for teenagers was well ahead of the times. Sunday evening youth meetings, which he directed, drew well over a hundred young people. Trips were planned to visit other churches in Middle Tennessee for youth-oriented activities. One of the reasons many new familiesplaced membership was to expose their children to him.

One incident illustrates his intensity. Brother Collins had insomnia. My father was in the home furnishings business. One morning Brother Collins told his wife, "Ruth, call Brown and have him carpet our bedroom. When I am awake and walk the floor it's cold. The carpet will be warm." It is my opinion that many of those sleepless nights were the result of his care and concern for others.

James Vandiver

* * *

Willard Collins and I have been warm personal friends since 1939. When he and his new bride, Ruth Morris, moved to Old Hickory, Tennessee to work with the church, it was my happy privilege to help them unpack. I was a deacon at that time. Willard Collins, more than any other person, encouraged me to preach.

During the relatively short time Willard preached at Old Hickory, only about four years, the congregation grew rapidly. Some of the great Gospel Meetings were conducted during this period. Literally hundreds of people were baptized. During the mid-forties, Willard broadened the scope of his work when he joined forces with the leaders at David Lipscomb College in the expansion program. His work of preaching and traveling on behalf of the college during these forty intervening years have carried him into most of the states and into many foreign countries.

I firmly believe that Willard Collins has touched the lives of more people than any living person in the church today. When you consider his gospel meeting schedule over a forty-year period, and add to that his influence on students at DLC over that same period of time, you can begin to appreciate the extent of his influence.

I cherish our friendship through the years and salute him on the occasion of his retirement as president of David Lipscomb College in August of 1986.

Joe Sanders

* * *

Willard Collins is no small man and by the hundreds of thousands we have been blessed by his stature.

Willard Collins is a big man in the alertness of his mind. Few grasp facts more readily or seek them more eagerly.

Willard Collins is a big man in his ability to see in clear execution that which exists only as a dream. He organizes with extraordinary efficiency.

Willard Collins is a big man in his ability to communicate. Few can inspire and motivate with words as well as he. The effectiveness of his preaching bears tremendous testimony to the power of his communication.

Willard Collins is a big man in his ability to follow. He bends to make a good team member.

Willard Collins is a big man in his ability to lead. Lipscomb's continued growth and positive spirit is a monument to this fact.

Willard Collins is a big man in his relations with others. He is neither small nor petty, and by his genuineness calls forth the best in others.

Willard Collins is a big man in his ability to work. His capacity for toiling long hours is well known.

Willard Collins is a big man in moral intent. His desire to be right and to do right shines through.

Willard Collins is a big man in faith. Beyond his own abilities, he is genuinely dependent upon the acts of the God in whom he trusts.

Willard Collins has blessed us out of the bigness of his spirit. His is a dimension of the soul we gladly salute.

James O. Baird
President Emeritus
Oklahoma Christian College

* * *

Willard Collins is one of the great men of our generation and to know him is to understand why this is true. Across the years it has been my privilege to see him excel in whatever he was doing. As vice-president and president of David Lipscomb College his work and life will influencefor good generations that will come after him. Brother Collins was first a preacher. During our years in Little Rock he came for several meetings. These meetings were greatly loved and successful in every way. He is one of the best loved men who came there for meetings.

Willard Collins has been one of our best friends for many years. There is no way to place a value on his friendship. He is warm and kind, generous, lovable and optimistic. I always feel better after being with him. It is my belief that some of his better days are yet to be because he will have more time for preaching and, after all, that is what he likes to do best.

Cleon Lyles

* * *

I was single in college in Oklahoma. Willard Collins was single in then far-away Tennessee. He came to Prairie Hill in Oklahoma to conduct his first Gospel meeting and I—being somewhat older— was holding meetings in Comanche nearby. Both churches bragged on our early preaching and thus helped us along the way. We sent messages back and forth but didn't meet until the Summer of 1940 in Shawnee where we had moved and that very night after his sermon we invited him over for homemade ice cream. He and Ruth became bosom friends to us. Meeting after meeting we had together in various places staying always in the other's home. Our two girls grew up together. We have movies of those good days. For years I stayed in their home in Nashville while attending board meetings in their city or in speaking at Lipscomb. Mama used to often say: "When young you make friends and when old you make acquaintances." Guille and I often relive in our memories those good days of yore with Willard and Ruth. No better friends have we ever had. We have talked together often of our retirements and that just maybe we can be together more.

Few men have contributed as much to the Cause of Christ and

to the educating of young men and women to be genuinely Christian as has Willard Collins, a truly genuinely Christian leader.

Hulen L. Jackson

* * *

One of the great blessings of my life has been my association with Willard Collins. I have no closer friends than Willard and Ruth. Our association began in 1934 at David Lipscomb. My appreciation for him has grown from that day until now.

I appreciate Willard for his genuineness. He is what he is. The honors that have been bestowed upon him, and all deserved, have not changed him from the same Christian gentleman he was when I first met him.

I appreciate him for his faithfulness with balance. I have never known him to sacrifice truth for popularity or to compromise his conviction of right. Not every man in his position has been able to do this. Yet while holding to truth and right he has never been given to extremes. This is a rare quality.

I appreciate him for his love of life. I know of no one that enjoys life more than Willard. One cannot be around him without his love of life rubbing off on one. He loves life more than grapes and there are few things he loves more than grapes. We are never together without laughing a great part of the time. He is like a ray of sunshine in a storm.

I appreciate him for his love. He loves God, the Bible and people. He has a special love for young people and they return his love. It is the highest compliment to be loved by boys and girls. This illustrates his being Christ like. Children loved Christ because he loved them.

I doubt is there is any one of his generation that has his persuasive power in the pulpit. He is a master in moving men to obey the gospel. I thank God that his providence brought me under his influence for good. My life will always be richer because of my association with Willard and Ruth Collins. They are two of God's great people.

Franklin Camp

* * *

You often make the statement, "I know that person quite well." I had made a similar statement about Willard Collins. However, I found that I really just began to know him as I became associated with him on the Board of Directors.

Willard became President of David Lipscomb College at a very critical and important time in its history. He did an outstanding work in replacing the confidence of the staff, faculty, students and the churches.

When Dr. Hooper asked me what I thought was one of his strongest characteristics, without hesitation I said "people." It never ceases to amaze me the number of people he knows. In our travels together he would always see someone he knew and immediately ask about each of their family by name.

Willard is a man who has depended on his team, as he calls his staff members, to carry on the day to day operations of the school.

One of the outstanding blessings of my life has been to be associated with and to work with Willard Collins.

Tom McMeen
Chairman of the
Board of Directors
David Lipscomb College

* * *

From the first day that I met Willard Collins many years ago, in his earliest days at David Lipscomb College, I have regarded him as being one of the finest Christian individuals I have known. Through the years I have been honored to count him as a good friend. His contribution to Christian education is one of the very greatest in our century. He has set the highest example of integrity, Christian commitment, and love for his fellow human beings. To a degree that is all too rarely seen, he has been able to maintain the strongest convictions and the kindest of dispositions at the same time.

The crowning achievement of his work as a preacher of the gospel and as a Christian educator has been his career as president of David Lipscomb College. When he took office the school faced a number of very serious challenges. The leadership that Willard Collins provided helped to move David Lipscomb College toward a much stronger financial position and to a greater stability in all of its operations. Major additions have been made to the physical plant, such as the Axel Swang business building. He has responded to the challenge with great success.

Although he is retiring from the presidency of David Lipscomb College, I confidently predict that he will continue to be most useful in the work of the church and in Christian education.

Howard A. White
President Emeritus
Pepperdine University

* * *

The names Willard and Ruth Collins conjure up many pleasant and meaningful memories for Peggy and me. Most precious of all is to recall the day he baptized one of our children. Such moments are poignant and significant in the life of a family. To share that time with a giant among our brotherhood such as Willard Collins was a unique treasure.

Willard's outstanding leadership, ever firm, ever convicted, has been an example to all who have known him. His strong yet gentle touch has molded David Lipscomb College through crucial years for Christian higher education. His success has been an example to all of us who seek to lead a Christian college or university in the Way.

In February 1985, Willard was the brother chosen to bring the keynote address at Abilene Christian University's annual Preachers-Elders-Deacons dinner, held each year in conjunction with Lectureship. On that particular evening, we announced the beginning of an 18.5 million dollar campaign to build the College of Biblical Studies here at ACU. It was an historic evening—perhaps the most important in our 80-year history. Willard's inimitable voice boomed through the packed hall, stirring the hearts of each man present.

To Willard, we offer our deepest gratitude and respect,our fondest personal affection, and our best wishes for many fulfilling years ahead of service in the Lord's Kingdom.

Sincerely,
Bill and Peggy Teague
President
Abilene Christian University

* * *

Dear Willard and Ruth,

We love and appreciate you both very much and are grateful for your many years of friendship and service in Christian education and in the Lord's kingdom. Your lives have been exemplary and you have been great models for the young people who have been under your care. There is no way to measure the amount of good that you have accomplished and the lasting influence which you have had on multitudes of people. Thank you for being warm, friendly and loving. The world needs people who have these characteristics and who are willing to give themselves in service unto others.

We appreciate your character and integrity and the fact that people have had great confidence in you. Your lives have been above reproach and this has helped you to be leaders at Lipscomb and in the church.

We are grateful for your dedication and your hard work. You have spent countless hours in service when you may have enjoyed life and have pursued an easier course. This has been a blessing to others and a wonderful example to those who have worked with you.

Thank you for having a great spirit that exudes confidence and victory in Jesus and love for His kingdom. We believe that this is one reason for your success in so many areas. We have truly enjoyed our association and work together and pray God's blessings upon you as you complete one facet of your work—the leadership of David LipscombCollege. May the Lord continue to bless you and use you in His service.

Sincerely yours,
Louise and Clifton Ganus, Jr.
President
Harding University

* * *

Willard Collins is one of the great men of my experience. I think it was love at first sight. I had enrolled as a Lipscomb freshman from Fort Worth and hit the campus like a Texas tornado. In those days, Brother Collins ran everything relating to student affairs.

In these days of complex administration, it is hard to believe that he actually was Dean of Men and Dean of Women; that he was in charge of student housing, intramurals and all extracurricular activities; and that he was the organizer and inspiration for the student government operations. If somebody got sent home it was Willard who had to do it, and when one of us did something right he was the first to beam his congratulations!

So there he was, that first day in September, 1954, at freshman orientation, booming out instructions from the auditorium stage. His hair was black and slicked back, his pinstriped suit sharply pressed and accented with a crisp white shirt and bright silk tie with a flashy stickpin. He looked for all the world like a member of the Chicago Mafia. At first glance, he even had a bit of a hard look; but what a marshmallow inside.

In those days, Willard Collins was probably the most popular gospel preacher on the Lipscomb faculty. Out in the churches, the ordinary people most loved to hear him. He had to make the decision in those days, perhaps unwittingly, between committing himself more fully to preaching or giving his life to David Lipscomb College. He has always been a great preacher, but if that had been his only work he probably would have been the very greatest. He certainly had that precious gift of preaching which attracted all of us interested in preaching so much to him. But the greatest attraction was his great, wonderful heart, his love, warmth, kindness, gentleness, goodness, sincerity, and integrity. Willard had the authentic ability to be genuinely interested in each and every student as an individual person.

And he was more than merely interested. He could also remember the minute, and frequently embarrassing, details about one's life and conduct. But with brother Collins you always knew that it was real, that he truly cared, and that he always would. Willard is like Christ in many ways, but one of the most conspicuous is his whole-hearted love of every individual, from the highest to the lowest.

It was Willard who provided me with my earliest strategic guidance as President of the freshman class. Later, after Gay and I were married, it was Willard who got me my first regular preaching job at Cherry Grove, Kentucky. And, it was Willard who gave me the biggest hug on graduation day.

After graduating, Willard and Ruth visited Gay and me in Albuquerque, where we were preaching. Our friendship has grown stronger through these years since Lipscomb.

What a role model he has been! Undoubtedly, Willard Collins was personally a part of the inspiration for me to go on to graduate school and eventually get into the administration of higher education. It certainly is not a coincidence that my first job at Pepperdine University in 1960 was as Dean of Students—the very kind of role Willard played when I was a student at Lipscomb.

It is a thrill to know one who is both such a great man and also such a good man. For a whole generation of us, the quintessence of the spirit of David Lipscomb College is not a song, or an idea, or a building, but a man. And his name is Willard Collins.

William S. Banowsky
Class of 1958

* * *

When Batsell Barrett and I arrived in Nashville in 1945 to begin work with David Lipscomb College, Willard and Ruth Collins were among the first to welcome us.

Willard's obvious love of the Lord, and of every good work for His church and for mankind, soon showed my husband that he was a person with whom it would be a joy to work in efforts to achieve the goals they shared. Through the years, as their friendship deepened, he felt that Willard was a person with whom he could discuss any decision of a personal nature that he faced, or any hope of his heart, or any problem needing solution. And when Batsell Barrett faced his own death, Willard Collins was one of the dear friends he hoped would be able to conduct his funeral service.

Since that time, Willard and Ruth—it is impossible to think of one without thinking of the other—have counselled with me, wept with me, laughed with me, and I am sure, prayed for me. I am grateful for the blessing of their friendship.

Wanda Roberts Baxter

* * *

I believe one of our richest blessings is our God-given ability to remember. My first memory of Willard was as the enthusiastic minister of the church in Old Hickory. With his leadership, this congregation enjoyed a phenomenal growth.

Our enduring friendship developed during the years that Willard was Vice President of David Lipscomb College and Ira was Professor of Speech and Bible.

Willard's glowing introductions were always a joy to hear. Frequently Ira would say, "You just haven't been introduced until you are introduced by Willard Collins. I would like to have him travel with me as an introducer."

The many times we met for lunch to share ideas and problems and encourage each other became known as "Crisis Luncheons." Ideas such as the television series *Know Your Bible*, *Five Golden Minutes*, and the *Amazing Grace Bible Class*, were created around the dinner table in the Collins home.It was Willard who encouraged Ira to write *The Madison Story* and *Balance*. He was a genuine friend to Ira and remains such to our entire family.

Willard and Ruth have lived as a team, with her serving as his help meet, rearing a good family, working faithfully in the church and diligently in Christian education.

Mrs. Ira North

* * *

Brother Collins, Dot and I respect and honor you as a Christian man of dignity. Being of the same County, you began to affect our lives early from the pulpits of Marshall County, Tennessee.

Your words of direction, instruction, and advice in our wedding ceremony, have lingered through the years. Our wedding ceremony was one of your very first. To your comment, "I must have done a good job, you are still together." We say, "Amen." Thank you for your continued encouragement in every phase of life.

Brother Collins, we honor and respect you because of the priorities of your life. Your love for preaching the gospel, Christian education, and souls of all mankind has affected our lives from before our wedding day down to our grandchildren. We owe you so very, very much.

Much has been learned from you, Brother Collins. I have learned from you as I observed you in Campaigns for Christ, as I led singing for you in gospel meetings, as I observed you in children's classes in meetings, as you preached in Campaigns and gospel meetings where I was the local preacher and as I have read from your pen.

When I first entered Lipscomb College you met with the preacher students on Monday nights; I learned much from you. You advised the young preachers, "Do the Work, salaries and raises will take care of themselves, DO THE WORK!" I respect you for the many times you gave me sound advice.

Maurice O'Neal

* * *

My first recollections of Brother Collins go back to my student days. When I entered Lipscomb as a freshman in the fall of 1949, Brother Collins was Vice President of the College and a teacher of Bible. It was my privilege to have been in his Bible class during my senior year.

After my graduation from Lipscomb, our paths crossed again in 1958 when he came to the Vultee Church of Christ in Nashville, Tennessee, for a gospel meeting. Those of us who worked and worshipped at the Vultee church had put forth a great deal of preparation for this meeting, but the crowds coming to hear Willard Collins were far beyond our expectations. As a matter of fact, the crowds outgrew the building and we were forced to open the doors and windows, place speakers outside and rent a tent to accommodate the audience. This particular effort was the best of its kind in which I have had the privilege of working.

In the fall of 1958 I began my first year as a teacher at David Lipscomb College, and as the years passed Brother Collins invited me to serve on the school's lecture committee. This was truly a learning experience for me as I was given the privilege of observing him develop a unique lecture series. In my opinion, the June lectures at Lipscomb belong to Willard Collins. Many of the same people attend this series year after year and most of them look forward to the first Monday night where he meets and greets the audience by states. His unique personality shines forth in a manner that makes the evening a delight.

It has also been my privilege to see Brother Collins in action as Chairman of the Student Affairs Committee of Lipscomb. This committee serves as the discipline committee and, as such, meets with students and parents when student problems develop. In this setting the concern, fairness, and dedication of the man has been seen by literally hundreds fo people.

In these settings, and others like them, I have learned much from Brother Collins.

Carl McKelvey

* * *

It is a rare administrator who is loved by all and about whom no unkind words can be recalled, but Brother Collins is that kind of person. I'm thankful his life has touched mine and that I can call him my friend.

Jim Ward
Library

* * *

As a youngster, I cleaned his furnace of clinkers. As a Lipscomb teacher I have enjoyed the clinkers he pulled in chapel and in correspondence. He is a unique individual, a man of integrity and deep sensitivity. He has made us want to work together as a team.

John C. Hutcheson, Jr.
Art

* * *

I feel a special kinship to Brother Collins since I joined the Lipscomb family the same year he became president. It has been a joy to see the growth of the college both spiritually and in attitude of the entire campus community. Brother Collins is responsible in large part for these changes.

Larry Griffith
Music

* * *

As a "short-timer" I sense that I have been privileged to be here during the "Golden Era of Lipscomb" under your leadership. You have made this Texan feel that he has a home in Tennessee, and he is forever grateful.

Jim Jackson
Music

* * *

Our brother, Willard Collins, continues to illuminate the joy and optimism which result from a life of serving and loving. He humbly allows Christ's light to shine through him and to warm others.

Charles H. McVey, Jr.
Languages

195

* * *

Willard Collins: A rare combination of the strength of manly leadership and the simple beauty of childlike faith in Jesus Christ.

Howard Horton
Bible

* * *

Willard Collins—a true neighbor, a faithful friend, an outstanding Christian, and an effective leader in Christian education, who bridged the gap between failure and success.

Axel W. Swang
Business

* * *

Sincere thanks for baptizing me, for bringing me to Lipscomb, and for serving us so well for so many years.

Norman Keener
Psychology

* * *

A faithful friend "come fair or foul."

Gladys Gooch
Languages

* * *

President Collins is a man secure enough to prefer the team concept of administration, humble enough to seek and follow the advice of others, and Christian enough to admit his limitations. These great qualities have made him an excellent president.

Clyde M. Miller
Bible

* * *

I fondly think of Brother Collins as an eternal optimist with a tremendous sense of humor.

Hollis Todd
Sociology

"That is all!"

Bison Day 1980

Mark McInteer presents the Christian Leadership Award to Collins on behalf of *20th Century Christian.*

A bucketful of change from the August Class of 1979

INDEX

199